The
Kabbalah Reiki Manual

Liliana Cisneros

The Kabbalah Manual © Mum Lily (Liliana Cisneros) 2024

ISBN: 978-1-923163-63-8 (Paperback)

This book is the intellectual property of Mum Lily, and it is protected by the copyright laws of Australia and, by extension, other countries. The contents herein, including text and images, may not be reproduced, or transmitted in any form or by any means—electronic, mechanical, photocopying, recording, or otherwise—without prior written permission from the publisher, except for brief quotations in book reviews or scholarly contexts, in accordance with the provisions of the Copyright Act.

While "The Kabbalah Manual" is presented with the intention of offering information of a reliable nature, it is provided with the understanding that the author and publisher are not engaged in rendering legal, financial, or other professional services. If expert assistance is required, please seek the services of a competent professional.

The publisher does not endorse and is not responsible for any third-party services that may be mentioned in this book. Use of these services should be based on your own due diligence, and you agree that the author and the publisher are not liable for any success or failure that is directly or indirectly related to the purchase and use of our information, products, and services reviewed or advertised.

Published in Australia by Mum Lily

www.mumlily.com
www.casaalhambra.com.au

Mum Lily Teaches
Liliana Alva de Cisneros
Casa Alhambra

Mum Lily Teaches

Mum Lily Teaches
Casa Alhambra

askmumlily@gmail.com
casaalhambra@outlook.com

77 Vulture Street – West End – QLD – 4101 – Australia

0415-422-007

Introduction

Welcome to the transformative world of Kabbalah Reiki, a spiritual journey that harmonizes the ancient wisdom of Kabbalah with the healing energies of Reiki. This manual is designed for seekers who are ready to explore the profound connections between universal life force energy and the mystical teachings of the Kabbalistic Tree of Life.

Kabbalah, the esoteric school of thought originating in Judaism, offers deep insights into the nature of the divine, the universe, and the human soul. Reiki, a Japanese technique for stress reduction and relaxation, channels healing energy through the hands, promoting healing and balance. By integrating these two powerful traditions, Kabbalah Reiki emerges as a unique spiritual practice that enhances well-being on all levels—physical, emotional, and spiritual.

As you journey through this manual, you will be guided through the fundamental concepts of Kabbalah and Reiki, learning how to apply these in your healing practice to achieve deeper spiritual connections and promote holistic healing in yourself and others. This journey is not just about learning techniques, but about evolving spiritually and discovering your true potential.

Thank you for choosing this path. May your study of Kabbalah Reiki open new doors of understanding and bring profound healing to your life and that of those you touch.

Table of Contents

Introduction

Part I: Foundations of Kabbalah Reiki   1

- Kabbalah and Kabbalah Reiki   3
- Foundational Concepts: 5
  - Practices Associated with Kabbalah   5
  - Important Kabbalistic Texts   6
  - History of Kabbalah   7
  - Types of Kabbalah   8
  - Principles of Reiki   9
  - History of Reiki   10

Part II: The Mystical Framework   11

- The Angelic and Mystical Realms: 13
  - A History of Angels   13
  - The Tree of Life   14
  - The Angelic Realm   18
  - The Archangel Seals   24

Part III: Core Practices and Techniques   25

- Kabbalah Reiki Practices: 27
  - Invocating the Archangels   27
  - The Angel Prayer of Protection   28
  - Hebrew Alphabet   29
  - The 72 Names of God   31
  - Thorough Procedure for Working with The 72 Names of God.   33
  - The 72 Names of God - Complete Chart   35
  - Reiki Symbols Used in Kabbalah Reiki   42

Part IV: Special Healing and Advanced Techniques   43

- Special Healing Techniques: 45
  - How to Release a Person from Black Magic   45
  - How to Clear Karma   46
  - How to Activate a Person's DNA   47
  - How to Do a General Healing   48
  - How to Do a Healing for Anxiety   49
  - How to Do a Healing for Depression   50
  - How to Do a Healing for Addictions   51
  - How to Call for a Miracle   52

☐ Soul Retrieval	53
☐ How to Do a Kabbalistic Soul Retrieval	55
☐ How to Do a Kabbalistic-Shamanic Soul Retrieval	56
☐ Giving a Kabbalah Reiki Treatment – Step by Step	60
☐ Ana Bekoach – The 42-letter Name of God	61
☐ Pitum HaKetoret - The Blending of the Incense	63
☐ The Aaronic Blessing	66
☐ Example of a Healing Session	67
☐ Recommended Morning Routine	69

Part V: The Seals of King Solomon — 71

☐ The Seals of King Solomon	73
☐ The 44 Seals	75
☐ The Seals of King Solomon – One Page Chart	76
☐ The Seals of the Sun	77
☐ The First Seal of the Sun	78
☐ The Seals of the Sun Chart	80
☐ The Seals of the Moon	84
☐ The Seals of the Moon Chart	85
☐ The Seals of Mars	88
☐ The Second Seal of Mars	89
☐ The Seals of Mars Chart	91
☐ The Seals of Mercury	95
☐ The Seals of Mercury Chart	96
☐ The Seals of Jupiter	99
☐ The Seals of Jupiter Chart	100
☐ The Seals of Venus	104
☐ The Seals of Venus Chart	105
☐ The Seals of Saturn	108
☐ The Seals of Saturn Chart	109
☐ The 72 Names of God and the King Solomon's Seals	113
☐ Summary Attunement and Activation of King Solomon's Seals	115
☐ The Seals of King Solomon - One Page Chart	124

Part VI: Merkabah Mysticism — 125

☐ What is the Merkabah?	127
☐ Historical Background	128
☐ The Significance of Merkabah in Spiritual Practices	128
☐ Techniques for Activating the Merkabah	128
☐ Applications of the Merkabah:	129
☐ Spiritual Ascension	129
☐ Healings	130

- Protection — 130
- Integration of the Self — 131
- Working with the Merkabah for Ascension – Step-by-Step Instructions. — 132
- Healing with the Merkabah: — 133
  - Physical Healing — 134
  - Emotional and Mental Healing — 134
  - Spiritual Healing — 134
  - Healing Through Dimensional Access — 135
  - Integration and Grounding — 135
- Advanced Visualization Techniques — 136
- Incorporating Sacred Geometry — 138
- Connection with Angelic Realms — 140
- Breathing Exercises and Mantras — 141
- Integration with Other Spiritual Practices — 144
- Ethical Considerations and Safety — 147

Part VII: Gematria — 149

What is Gematria? — 151
Principles of Gematria — 151
Applying Gematria in Kabbalah Reiki — 151
Gematria in Practice: Step-by-Step — 151
Case Studies: — 152
- Case Study 1: Healing with a Personal Name — 152
- Case Study 2: Focusing on a Significant Date — 152

Part VIII: Ethical Practice and Professional Development — 153

- Ethical Guidelines for Kabbalah Reiki — 155
- Setting Boundaries with Clients — 157

Part IX: Meditation, Lifestyle, and Continued Learning — 159

- Meditation and Visualization: — 161
  - Guided Practices for Kabbalah Reiki — 161
- Dietary and Lifestyle Recommendations — 164
- Continued Learning and Development — 166

Part X: Closing Remarks and Resources — 169

- Dear Beloved Souls — 171
- About Mum Lily — 173
- Contact Information — 175

Part I

Foundations of Kabbalah Reiki

Kabbalah and Kabbalah Reiki

Kabbalah is a mystical, magical, philosophical, and spiritual doctrine, through which God, The Creator, The Ein Sof, reveals Himself to His creation. It offers us a deeper understanding into the essence of The Creator and into the wisdom of His creative actions. Since The Creator is in everything, the study of Kabbalah is the study of everything and its connection with us.

The word Kabbalah means 'to receive', and that is exactly what it does. Kabbalah teaches us how to get close to the Divinity, how 'to receive Him', and finally, how to merge with Him, allowing for the perfection of the self.

The Kabbalah was originally taught by The Creator to the Angels, who in turn, taught it to mankind.

By studying Kabbalah, we learn to expand the borders of our natural senses, achieving what is known as 'the sixth sense'; that is, the ability to see and perceive beyond what our natural senses let us know. When we study Kabbalah, we connect with the deepest part of ourselves, bringing our inner light out, a light that is so powerful, that it can transform our reality. Kabbalah teaches us about the spiritual world. It helps us to define humanity's position in the universe, why we exist, why we were born, what the purpose of our life is, and where we will go after completing our life in this world.

Kabbalah is universal, and people from various points of view, philosophies, and even religions, have found great inspiration for their lives in it. Kabbalah has been kept secret for most of the time, a privilege of the few. However, we are now living at a time when wisdom and knowledge are becoming more readily available to everyone. And it is at this time that Kabbalah, with all the richness it brings, is available for you and me.

Kabbalah Reiki is a unique, wonderful healing modality that combines the miraculous, powerful secrets of Kabbalah with the power of Reiki. The result is a highly applicable, easy to use technique that is able to break through any barriers bringing healing and well-being. While Kabbalah on its own is supremely powerful. However, it is also very complex, and can take more than a lifetime to master it, and to know how to apply it in our lives. The aim of Kabbalah Reiki is to make Kabbalah more accessible to everyone. We are very pleased to present you with this amazing technique. The results that you will experience with it are life changing.

Foundational Concepts
Practices Associated with Kabbalah

- ☐ Working with the 72 Names of God
- ☐ The Sacred Magic of the Angels
- ☐ Sacred Geometry
- ☐ The Tree of Life
- ☐ Alchemy
- ☐ Gematria (Numerology)
- ☐ Astrology
- ☐ Tarot

Kabbalah is not a religion, but it does require the belief in a Higher Power. The goal of Kabbalah is not to follow laws and rituals, but rather to seek the divine within oneself to become closer to the Creator and allow greater insight into His creation.

Kabbalah is called the Western Mystery Tradition because it is the esoteric teaching behind Judaism, Islam, Christianity, as well as the Hermetic Mystery Schools. Understanding Kabbalah assists in better understanding the deeper concepts that these groups teach.

Important Kabbalistic Texts

- The Torah, also known as The First Five Books of Moses -

The Torah describes the History of Creation, the Garden of Eden, the Tree of Knowledge of Good and Evil, and the Tree of Life. Kabbalists regard the Torah as God's wisdom and seek in it for greater messages, by analysing even the smallest letters, the repeated words and their numerical values.

- The Zohar, also known as Book of Splendour -

This is probably the best-known Kabbalistic classic. This book, or rather collection of books includes teachings on Creation, numerology, reincarnation, descriptions of heaven and the seven palaces of the Garden of Eden, and the secret of divinity.

- Sefer Yetzirah, also known as Book of Creation, or Book of Formation -

It deals with the study of the origin and evolution of The Universe, and the symbolism of numbers and letters.

- Sefer Raziel, also known as the Book of Raziel, the Angel -

It is a book dealing with Kabbalistic Magic. It contains teachings on angelology, magical uses of the zodiac, gematria, names of God, protective spells, and a method of writing magical healing amulets.

- Sefer Ha-Razim, also known as Book of Secrets -

This is also a book of Kabbalistic Magic, supposedly given to Noah by the angel Raziel, and passed down throughout history to King Solomon. It is believed that this knowledge was the source of his wisdom and his magical powers. It talks about angels and their ability to perform supernatural deeds. It contains a list of the angels along with instructions to perform magical rites.

History of Kabbalah

Kabbalah was originally taught by *The Creator* to the *Angels* in the Heavenly Realm.

Later on, *Archangel Rahuel (also known as Archangel Ratziel)*, who is the Archangel of Wisdom, taught Kabbalah to *Adam*, as a way to assist mankind regain the Garden of Eden. That is, The Creator sent His Wisdom to mankind to assist them regain their former glory, their former connection to Divinity.

Adam then passed the Kabbalah to his son *Seth*, who then passed it to *Enoch*, and then to *Noah*, then to *Abraham*. The Kabbalah then went into Egypt when Abraham's descendants became enslaved in Egypt. The Kabbalah went then to *Moses* who in turn, passed it onto *Joshua*, until it reached 'the Men of the Great Assembly'. This means that around the 10th century BCE, Kabbalah became an open knowledge, practiced by over a million people in ancient Israel. Foreign invasions to Israel brought the Kabbalah to the civilizations where they went, such as *Babylon* and *Chaldea*.

Later, Kabbalah was taught and practiced at the 'School of Prophets' that *Samuel* founded at Mount Carmel. This school developed into the *Essenes*, which continued up through the time of Jesus. It is believed that *Jesus* was trained in Kabbalah, and that He received this training from the Essenes. The Essenes possessed the knowledge of an important aspect of Kabbalah called *B'reshit Mysticism*, also known as Creation Mysticism, which contains secrets of the creation of the universe. The Essenes were also in possession of The First Book of Enoch, which contained the main elements of Kabbalah.

After the destruction of the Second Temple in Jerusalem in 70 AD, Kabbalah reappeared under the name of *Merkabah Mysticism*, also known as Chariot Mysticism. Merkabah Mysticism emphasised on how to ascend through the spiritual realms or palaces, until reaching the Throne of God, with the intension of gaining a closer connection with the Divine, and getting insight into heavenly mysteries

Kabbalah appeared in Southern *France* around 1200 (12 hundred), spreading to Northern *Spain*. A renowned Kabbalists of this time is Isaac Luria. Kabbalah also became popular in the *Christian* world between the 1200 (12 hundred) to 1500. After the expulsion of the Jews from Spain in 1492, many Jews moved to the Holy Land, where Kabbalah had the opportunity to flourish again. *Hermetic Qabalah* gained strength since the 16th century. Hermetic Qabalah is the underlying philosophy and framework for magical societies such as the Golden Dawn.

The *20th Century* has seen a revival of Kabbalah among many groups. It has seen the scholarly study of Kabbalah, where research on a large scale and application of its proven methods have been undertaken, particularly by Professor Gershom Scholem.

Types of Kabbalah

Nowadays, we can find three main types of Kabbalah, in accordance with the groups they are associated with. You may find Kabbalah written with a K, or with a C, or with a Q, depending on which type of Kabbalah they are referring.

The Orthodox Jewish Kabbalah.-

This is the most traditional type of Kabbalah.
It includes what is known as *Experimental Kabbalah*. That is, the search for mystical experiences through contemplation, meditation, and ecstatic (out of body) experiences.

And also, what is known as *Practical Kabbalah*. This is a form of magic and relates to altering and influencing the course of nature, using the Divine Names, magical seals and other mystical exercises.

The Kabbalah of the Famous.-

This is the Kabbalah of the Kabbalah Centre in New York, USA. It mixes traditional Kabbalah teachings with New Age concepts. This type of Kabbalah is known due to its popularity with celebrities such as Madonna, Gwyneth Paltrow, Demi Moore, among others.

Christian Cabbala.-

Christian Cabala was popular during the Renaissance. It interpreted its doctrines to fit into the Christian dogma. Christian Cabbala is not currently very popular.

Hermetic Qabalah.-

Hermetic Qabalah combines Kabbalah with the teachings of the famous Hermes Trismegistus, plus the disciplines of astrology, and alchemy. Hermetic Qabalah is the underlying philosophy for magical societies such as the Golden Dawn.

Principles of Reiki

Reiki is a holistic healing practice that originated in Japan, founded by Mikao Usui in the early 20th century. It is grounded in the belief that universal energy can be harnessed and transmitted through the hands of a practitioner, facilitating the body's natural healing processes. Central to Reiki are its five guiding principles, which serve as a moral compass for practitioners, promoting spiritual and emotional well-being. These principles are often recited at the beginning of the day and during Reiki sessions to help individuals cultivate inner peace and balance. They include:

1. **Just for today, I will not be angry.**
   Anger is viewed as a blockage to energy flow and a barrier to healing. This principle encourages individuals to release anger, fostering a state of calm and serenity.

2. **Just for today, I will not worry.**
   Worry is another emotion that impedes the free flow of energy. Practitioners are encouraged to trust in the process and maintain a mindset of positivity and openness.

3. **Just for today, I will be grateful.**
   Gratitude expands one's focus on positive emotions and abundance, which supports healing and energy flow. Practitioners are urged to appreciate the blessings in their lives, fostering a sense of contentment and peace.

4. **Just for today, I will do my work honestly.**
   Honesty in one's actions and work cultivates integrity and authenticity, essential qualities for a Reiki practitioner. This principle emphasizes the importance of sincerity in all dealings, which enhances the practitioner's channeling abilities.

5. **Just for today, I will be kind to every living thing.**
   Kindness reinforces the interconnectedness of all beings and aligns practitioners with Reiki's nurturing aspect. It promotes compassion and empathy, which are vital for healing oneself and others.

By adhering to these principles, Reiki practitioners strive not only to heal others but also to foster their personal growth and spiritual development. These principles underscore the belief in Reiki as a life path, not just a healing tool, encouraging practitioners to live in harmony with the universe and those around them.

History of Reiki

Even though energy healing is a very ancient practice, Reiki was rediscovered and revived by the Japanese Christian monk Dr Mikao Usui in the 19th century.

Mikao Usui was the Principal of a Christian Seminary in Kyoto, Japan. Usui felt challenged in his faith when his students pointed out their inability to replicate Jesus' miracles, as explained in the Bible. They requested Usui to demonstrate Jesus' healing power before them. However, Usui could not do so, which propelled him to look further into this matter. Usui thought he might be more likely to find the key to his Christian question in a Christian country. This is how he ended up in America after resigning from his position in Japan.

Usui became a Doctor of Theology at the University of Chicago. However, he was none the wiser about replicating the hands-on healings he had read about in the Bible.

Usui kept searching. He searched the Chinese scripts and the Holy Writings in India but to no avail. Finally, Usui returned to Japan, where he discovered the Sanskrit formulas and symbols in old Buddhist Sutras, which seemed to hold the answers to his quest.

After fasting for 21 days and meditating on the Sutras, Usui was hit by a light beam in the centre of his forehead. He saw some Sanskrit symbols in front of him glowing. These symbols then became the foundations of Usui's system of Reiki. After this experience, Usui was able to experience some miracles as he began to practice his Reiki healing on the beggars of Kyoto. This became the beginning of a new chapter in Usui's life, where he started teaching Reiki to other people throughout Japan.

Upon his death, Mikao Usui was succeeded by Dr. Chijaro Hayashi, one of his most excellent collaborators. Hayashi was, in turn, followed by Madame Hawayo Takata (who was apparently cured of terminal cancer through Reiki treatments). Madame Takata lived, healed, and trained other Reiki healers in Hawaii for many years. She trained a total of 22 Masters in the US and Canada. Nowadays, Reiki is practised all over the world by thousands of people.

The Reiki system we teach in this course is known as the 'Usui Method of Reiki', named after its founder. It is a highly regarded system, considered the traditional Reiki system. Other Reiki systems include Angelic Reiki, Shamanic Reiki, Crystal Reiki, and Kabbalah Reiki, to name just a few.

Part II

The Mystical Framework

The Angelic and Mystical Realms
A History of Angels

In the beginning there was God. God is the original energy source of everything. He is infinite and has always existed. God wanting to enrich His experiences, His knowledge and wisdom, decided to expand Himself everywhere and off He went, to explore and create and learn. This action could be seen as the Sun sending its rays out, as waves of love, light and wisdom.

After stablishing His angelic realm, God invited and involved His angelic beings to be His co-creators in creating the rest of the universe. It was in this way, that the various galaxies, solar systems and planets were created, including our planet Earth.

In the angelic beings, we have a wonderful host of powerful spiritual friends willing and ready to help us with their wisdom, power, and love. The Angelic Realm is highly organized. We will be able to appreciate their organization in the Tree of Life.

> ▶ YouTube The Angels - 14th of March - Lily Wisdom of the Merkabah (Mum Lily Teaches)

The Tree of Life

In a *macrocosm* level, 'The Tree of Life' is a symbolic diagram that explains the design of the Universe and how it works. Here we find the four worlds, the position of the various angelic beings, their ruling Archangels, what they represent, and their relationship to the planets. This knowledge is very relevant in Kabbalah Reiki, as Kabbalah works with the Angelic Realm.

In a *microcosm level*, 'The Tree of Life', represents our path in life. The structure of the Tree represents the ideal design for each human being, one in the image of God. It shows us pathways from which to move through in order to achieve our highest potential.

At the head of the Tree of Life are:
Ein: The Eternal, The Endless One, Source, God
Ein Sof: The Eternal Light
Ein Sof Aur: The Light that emanates from the Eternal Light.

This indicates that it all starts with God, who in order to manifest Himself/Herself into existance, and in order to acquire experiences and really live and love, disperses Himself/Herself through the various spheres of the Tree of Life.

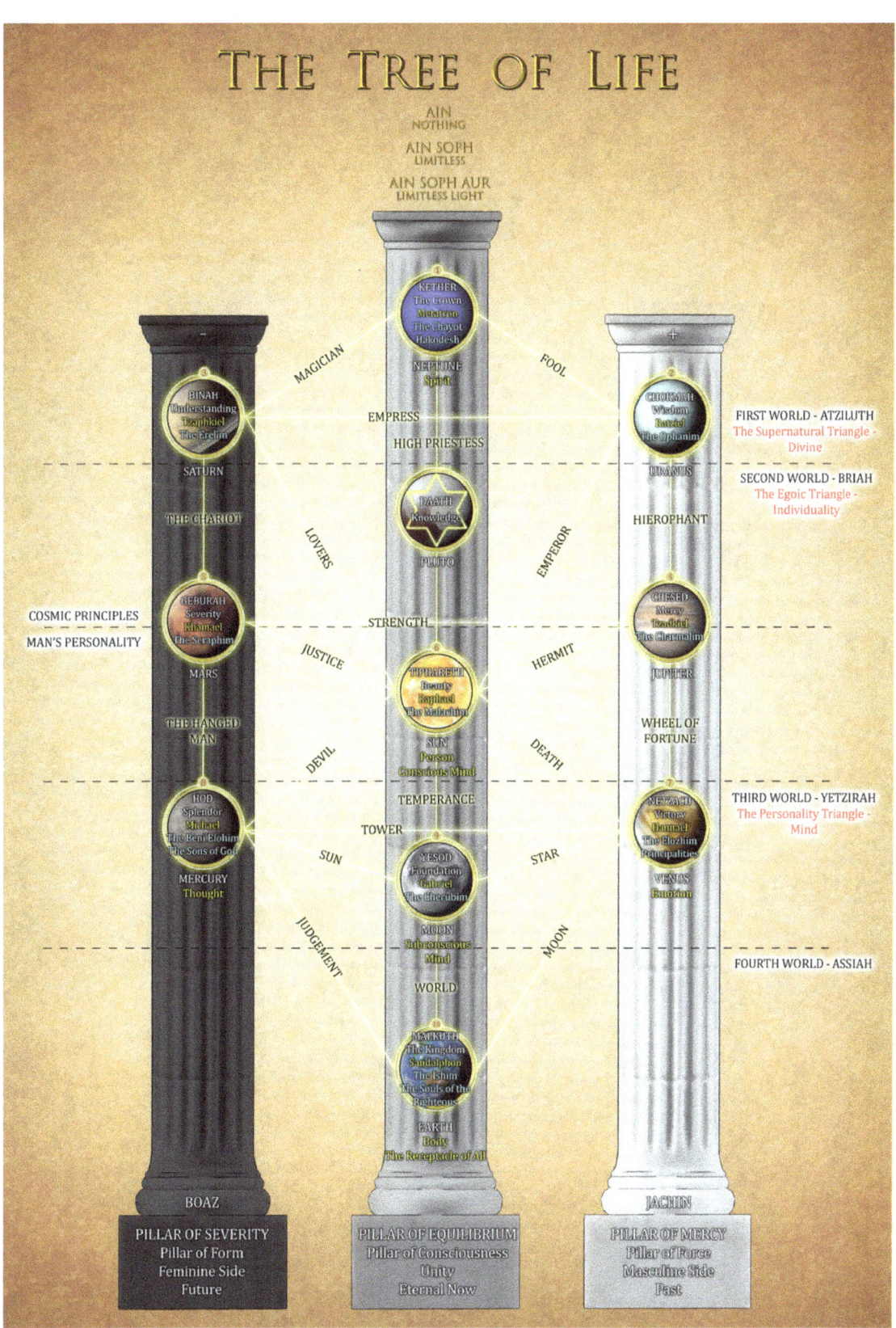

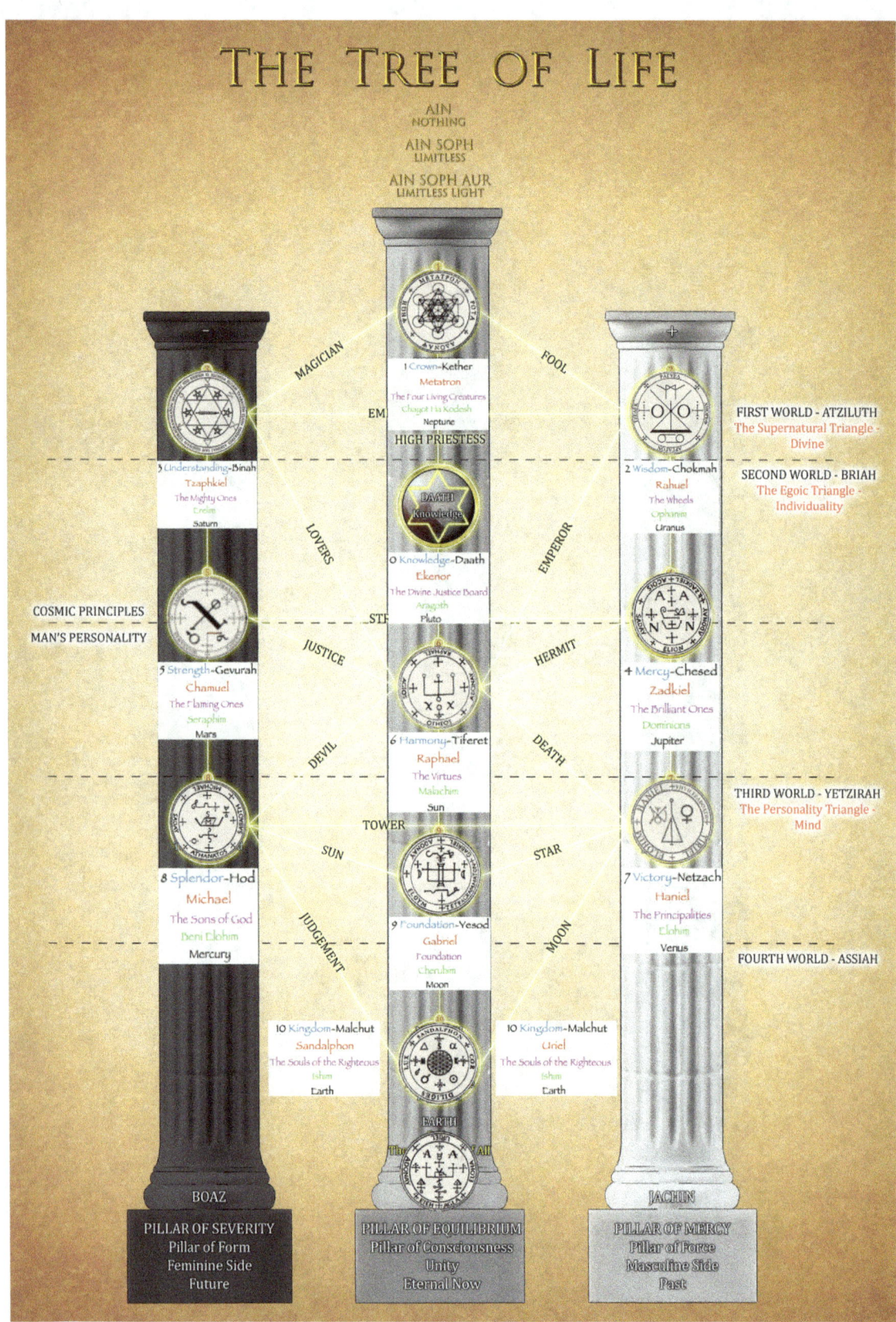

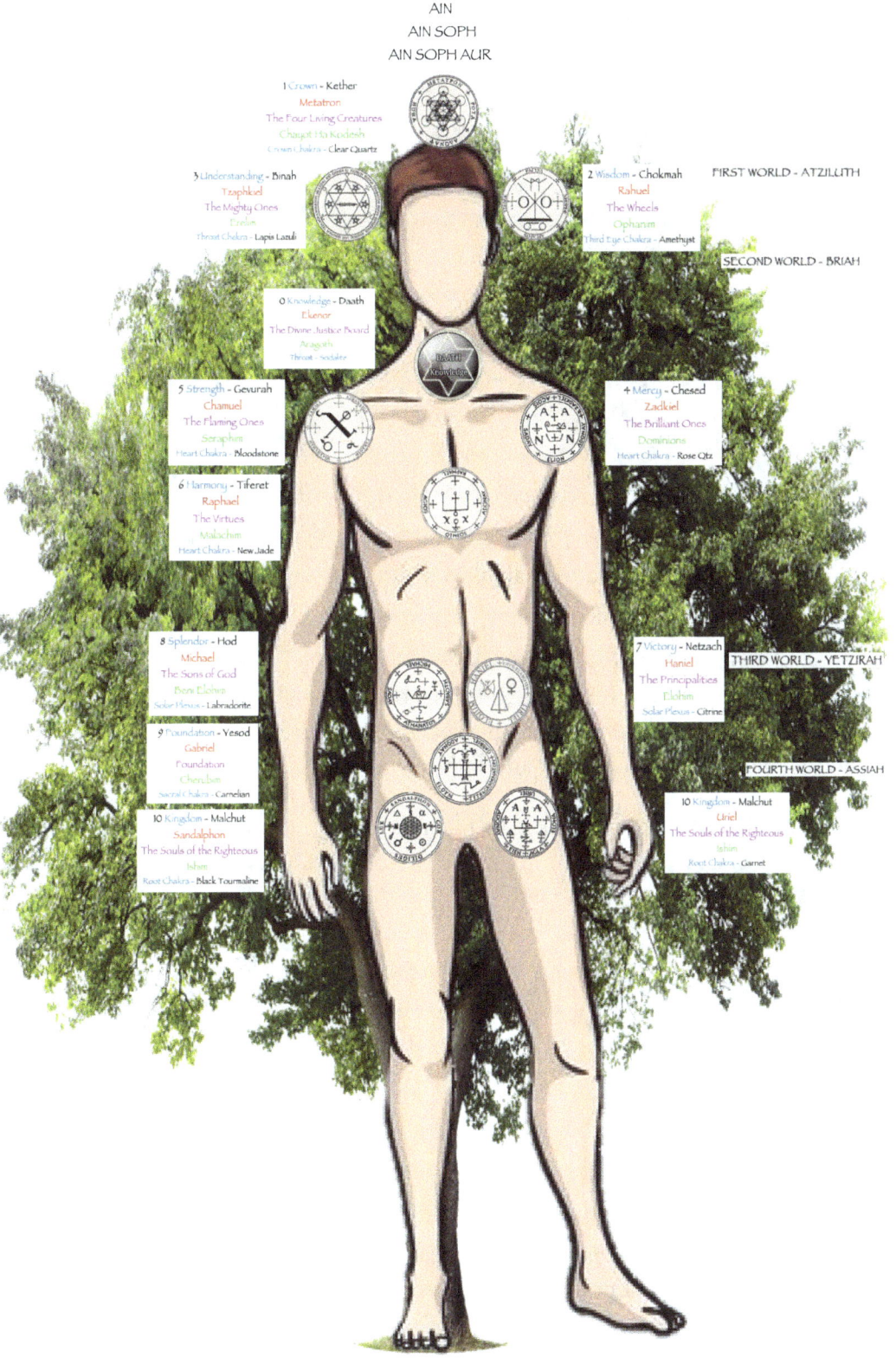

The Angelic Realm

Let's now talk about the Angelic Beings, and their place in the Tree of Life:

1- *'The Four Living Creatures', or 'Chayot Ha Kodesh'* –

They are the Supreme Order of Angels. They hold up The Creator's Throne and the Earth in place. They are in the emanation of *The Crown (Kether)* in the Tree of Life and are led by *Archangel Metatron*.

Archangel Metatron. 'The Angel of Life'. Metatron is the greatest angelic being, second in command only to God. He holds within its being-ness all the other Archangels and Angels. He presides over all the archangels and guards the Divine Throne. He acts as an intermediary between heavenly and lower worlds.

2- *'The Wheels', or 'Ophanim' in Hebrew* –

They are known for their wisdom and are the ones that facilitate the movement of the Merkabah - Chariot of God. They are positioned in the emanation of *Wisdom (Chokmah)* in the Tree of Life. They are led by *Archangel Rahuel (Ratziel)*.

Archangel Rahuel (Ratziel). 'Friend of the Creator'. Rahuel reveals Divine mysteries and helps people to acquire more wisdom. He helps people to incorporate knowledge into their lives in practical ways. Rahuel is also the Archangel of Harmony and Relationships. He supports family unity.

3- *'The Mighty Ones', or 'Erelim' in Hebrew –*

They are the agents of earthly justice and are known for their courage and understanding. They are positioned in the emanation of *Understanding (Binah)* in the Tree of Life. They are led by *Archangel Tzaphkiel*.

Archangel Tzaphkiel. Tzaphkiel is the Archangel of compassion and understanding, who helps us with forgiveness and unconditional love. It represents the feminine aspect of Creation, emanating unconditional love, forgiveness, non-judgement and compassion.

4- *'The Brilliant Ones', 'Dominions', or 'Chasmalim' –*

They are known for their love, kindness, and grace. They decide the success or failure of nations. They are positioned in the emanation of *Mercy (Chesed)* in the Tree of Life. They are led by *Archangel Zadkiel*.

Archangel Zadkiel. 'The Merciful'. Archangel Zadkiel sends God's mercy throughout the universe giving people the confidence that The Creator will answer their prayers according to what's truly best. Zadkiel brings joy, benevolence, freedom, and prosperity.

5- 'The Flaming Ones', or 'Seraphim' –

They embody the light, love, justice and fire of God, inspiring others to do the same. They surround God's Throne. They are positioned in the emanation of *Strength (Gevurah)* in the Tree of Life. They are led by *Archangel Chamuel*.

Archangel Chamuel. 'The Courageous'. Chamuel is the Archangel of peaceful relationships. He offers us strength, courage and peace through times of severity. Chamuel has omniscient vision, and can see the connection between everyone and everything, and can see the solution to every problem.

6- 'The Virtues', 'The Kings' or 'Malachim' –

They are brilliant, beautiful and are usually in a group. They are the angels of miracles, and encouragement. The Malachim are positioned in the emanation of *Harmony (Tiferet)* in the Tree of Life. They are led by *Archangel Raphael*.

Archangel Raphael. 'The Healer'. Raphael is the Healing Archangel, who heals physically, mentally, spiritually and even financially. He warns of danger and encourages devotion to causes. Raphael inspires musicians. He is one of the five angels who keep watch over both the celestial and terrestrial worlds.

7- 'The Principalities', or 'Elohim' –

They are committed to the victory of good over evil. They are the guardians of the nations and the leaders of the world. They are positioned in the emanation of *Victory (Netzach)* in the Tree of Life. They are led by *Archangel Haniel*.

Archangel Haniel. Archangel Haniel helps us to get closer to God and to other people. He brings us insights that bring us joy and happiness. Haniel brings together friends and lovers and supports them in their relationships. Haniel helps to enhance psychic powers, the use crystals and natural healing remedies.

8- 'The Sons of the Elohim', or 'Beni Elohim' –

They focus on giving glory to the Creator. They bring God's messages and command the armies of heaven. They are positioned in the emanation of *Splendor (Hod)* in the Tree of Life. They are led by *Archangel Michael*.

Archangel Michael. Archangel Michael is a mighty warrior angel. He is the Archangel of protection, courage, strength, and guidance. Michael is believed to be the highest-ranking warring angel in God's heavenly host. Michael protects us from psychic attacks.

9. 'The Archangels of Humanity', or 'Cherubim' –

They are full of wisdom and minister to us in every aspect of life. They are the Record Keepers of Heaven. They are positioned in the emanation of *Foundation (Yesod)* in the Tree of Life. They are led by *Archangel Gabriel*.

Archangel Gabriel. Gabriel is the Messanger Archangel, that brings us messages of hope and comfort. Gabriel brings inner strength, empathy, and forgiveness. Gabriel is the angel of fertility and assists mothers and mothers to be.

10. 'The Souls of the Righteous', or 'Ishim' –

They are the souls of just men who reside in the 5th Heaven. Their focus is on building God's kingdom on Earth. They are positioned in the emanation of *The Kingdom (Malchut)* in the Tree of Life. They are led by *Archangel Sandalphon and Archangel Uriel*.

Archangel Sandalphon. Sandalphon is the angel of prayer. He sends messages back and forth between God and man. Sandalphon weaves garlands out of human prayers and sends them to Heaven where Metatron receives them and gives them to The Creator.

Archangel Uriel. Archangel Uriel is the Light of God. He is the Archangel of Wisdom. Possibly Uriel's highest attribute is in that He is allowed to enter the presence of God; that is into God's Shekinah. That is why Uriel is also known as the 'Prince of The Presence'.

0. *'The Divine Justice Board', or 'Aragoth'* –

"The Divine Justice Board," also referred to as 'Aragoth,' is associated with the sphere of Daath, and translates as 'Knowledge, 'Doorway to God.' This board decides on a person's fate based on their karma or dharma. It is positioned in the emanation of Knowledge (Daath), the secret sphere.

Daath, is not typically included in the main sefirot (spheres) of the Kabbalistic Tree of Life because it is considered an invisible or hidden sephira. It symbolizes the conjunction of understanding (Binah) and wisdom (Chokhmah), and it serves as a doorway into deeper spiritual insight and divine mysteries.

Daath's positioning as a "Doorway to God" suggests it is a portal through which profound spiritual understanding and divine connection can be accessed. Within this context, "The Divine Justice Board" of Aragoth may be thought of as a metaphorical body that oversees spiritual law and order, determining a person's fate based on their karma or dharma. This idea illustrates how spiritual responsibility and cosmic justice are woven into the mystical teachings of the Tree of Life.

Archangel Ekenor: Ekenor is the Archangel of Power. He assists us to reach our highest potential, by reaching into the hidden knowledge of God's truths. Archangel Ekenor, might not be a traditionally recognized figure within classical religious texts but fits within the broader spiritual narratives that include celestial beings dedicated to assisting humans in reaching their spiritual potential. His role in accessing hidden knowledge aligns with Daath's thematic associations with hidden wisdom and the unveiling of divine truths.

This framework implies that mystical and esoteric teachings help mediate divine justice and empowerment, guiding individuals to their full potential through spiritual enlightenment and observance of universal laws.

 Metatron, The Merkabah & Merkabah Mysticism - January 16th 2021 - Lily Wisdom of the Merkabah
(Mum Lily Presents)

The Archangel Seals

1. Metatron
Clear Quartz

2. Rahuel
Amethyst

3. Tzaphkiel
Lapis Lazuli

4. Zadkiel
Rose Quartz

5. Chamuel
Bloodstone

6. Raphael
New Jade

7. Haniel
Citrine

8. Michael
Labradorite

9. Gabriel
Carnelian

10. Uriel
Golden Rutile

10. Sandalphon
Black Tourmaline

0. Ekenor
Sodalite

Part III

Core Practices and Techniques

Kabbalah Reiki Practices
Invocating the Archangels

When performing Kabbalah Reiki, you may choose to work with one single Archangel, or with several of them. Becoming familiar with the Archangels and their attributes is beneficial when selecting who to invoke. You may also choose to invoke all the Twelve Archangels of the Tree of Life at once. Invoking Archangels does not need to be complicated. Simply say:

'I now invoke Archangel(s)............... to assist with the healing of ....', or
'I now invoke the Twelve Archangels of the Tree of Life............ to assist with the healing of ....'

Remember to thank all the Archangels at the end of the healing.

The Angel Prayer of Protection

This is the prayer to make before a Kabbalah Reiki Treatment. In fact, it is recommended to make this prayer every morning before starting your day, to ensure you are protected and well-supported throughout your day.

B'sheim Hashem Elohei Yisrael,
mimini Michael,
umismoli Gavriel, Umilfanai Uriel
umeachorai Rafael,
V'al roshi Shechinat El

בְּשֵׁם הַשֵּׁם אֱלֹהֵי יִשְׂרָאֵל, מִימִינִי
מִיכָאֵל, וּמִשְּׂמֹאלִי גַּבְרִיאֵל, וּמִלְּפָנַי אוּרִיאֵל, וּמֵאֲחוֹרַי
רְפָאֵל, וְעַל רֹאשִׁי וְעַל רֹאשִׁי שְׁכִינַת אֵ-ל.

B'sheim Adonai Elohei Yisrael,
Mimini *Mihael*,
Miesmoli *Gavriel*,
Milefanai *Uriel*,
Meajorai *Rafael*,
V'al Roshi *Shechinat El*

In the name of the Creator God,
May *Michael* be at my right hand,
Gabriel at my left,
Uriel in front of me,
Raphael behind me,
And over my head *The Shekhinah Glory of God*, the Divine Presence of God

Gold Shield, Silver Shield

   B'Shaim Hashem-the Angel song
(YisraelbenDavid)

The Hebrew Alphabet

The Hebrew Alphabet is a very powerful tool. Each letter on its own is full of power and wonderful blessings. The Hebrew letters constitute the DNA of the Universe. It is believed that each Hebrew letter is in reality an Angelic Being. And that it is with these Angelic Beings that God created the world.

Becoming familiar with the Hebrew Alphabet is highly recommended, as it will help you with the pronunciation of the Names of God that we will utilizing in Kabbalah Reiki.

Learning the Hebrew letters can take some time. Do not let that discourage you. We will be providing the pronunciation to all the words you will need. However, we do encourage you to take the time to learn them at your own pace.

Hebrew is read from right to left. Therefore, we would start reading from Alef and end with Tav:

▶ YouTube Easy Hebrew Alphabet Song
(Iglesia En Buena Tierra)

Vowels are not part of the traditional Hebrew language. However, they were created to assist with reading. It is not essential to learn them for this course but are here as a reference:

	Long	Short
A (**a**rm)	ָ	ַ
E (p**e**n)	ֵ	ֶ
I (gr**ee**n)	ִי	ִ
O (yell**o**w)	וֹ	ָ
U (bl**u**e)	וּ	ֻ

▶ YouTube Hebrew Pronunciation - Hebrew Vowels
(Learn Hebrew with HebrewPod101.com)

The 72 Names of God

והו	ילי	סיט	עלם	מהש	ללה	אכא	כהת
הזי	אלד	לאו	ההע	יזל	מבה	הרי	הקם
לאו	כלי	לוו	פהל	נלך	ייי	מלה	וזהו
נתה	האא	ירת	שאה	ריי	אום	לכב	ושר
יוזו	להוז	כוק	מנד	אני	וזעם	רהע	ייז
ההה	מיכ	וול	ילה	סאל	ערי	עשל	מיה
והו	דני	הוש	עמם	ננא	נית	מבה	פוי
נמם	ייל	הרו	מצר	ומב	יהה	ענו	מוזי
דמב	מנק	איע	וזבו	ראה	יבמ	היי	מום

> ▶ YouTube — Names of God (Mum Lily Teaches)

The 72 Names of God are sacred letter combinations. Every 3-letter combination is a channel that connects us to a source of divine power. When we connect to these sacred names and assimilate them in our system, we can gain control over all aspects of our lives and change our lives for the better.

Each name carries unique qualities, designed to help us restore and cure the ills of the soul, body and mind, overcome crises, achieve abundance, joy, and happiness.

The 72 Names of God are so powerful that simply looking at them brings great blessings into our lives and the lives of those around us.

There are many ways to work with the 72 Names of God. The main ingredient is work with them with respect, with the intention of connecting with the angelic forces that guide them. Assimilating the 72 Names in our body, mind and spirit, on a daily basis, will deeply transform our life. The high frequencies of the 72 Names will penetrate each cell of our body, creating changes at the DNA level.

Below is the most thorough procedure to work with them. There is wisdom and reasons for each of the steps. It may seem like a long and complex procedure, at first. Yet, with practice, it becomes easy and second nature. We have attempted to present this procedure as accurate, yet as simple as possible. In order to accomplish this, we have limited our explanations to what is most needed.

The 72 Names of God is also known as the 216 Letter Name of God. The 216 Letter Name of God is really a 72 part Name, since it is a sequence of 72 triads of letters, all of which are derived from permutations on Exodus 14:19-21 (which itself is composed of three verses of 72 letters each).

To create the first triad, we put together the first letter of verse 14:19, the last letter of verse 14:20, and then the first letter of 14:21. To create the next triade, we put together the second letter of 14:19, the second to last of 14:20, and the second letter of 14:21. This continues untill all the letters are used up.

Thorough Procedure for Working with The 72 Names of God

Visualize or view the Hebrew letters and pronounce the words in green and blue.

As our example, we will be working with the Name for Healing:

מהש   Mem, Heh, Shin - Heals Spirit, Mind and Body. Also Heals Negative Situations. Heals Families, Businesses.

בָּרוּךְ אַתָּה יְיָ אֱלֹהֵינוּ מֶלֶךְ הָעוֹלָם

Baruch Ata Adonoy, Eloheinu Melech Ha-Olam.
Blessed are You, Oh Lord, God, King of the Universe.

'I call upon the presence of Archangels Metatron, Sandalphon and the Messiah to guide this process'.

לוו - Lamed, Vav, Vav. Connects us with God, removing any obstacles from our prayer.
ללה - Lamed, Lamed, Heh. Allows us to use any Name of God, at any time.
אראריתא - ARARITA. Protects our prayer. No negative angel can touch our prayer.
וְהֹיָהּ - VaHoYaHa. Opens the Doors of Eden, connecting us with God.
קָדוֹשׁ קָדוֹשׁ קָדוֹשׁ - Kadosh, Kadosh, Kadosh - Holy, Holy, Holy.

Visualize that you are in a Star of David.
Visualize another Star of David in front of you, with the Name of God selected.
Visualize a third Star of David with the person receiving the healing or blessing.

Visualize (view in your mind) the Name of God selected.
If you can't visualize it yet, view it.

Softly pronounce these letters: Mem, Hei, Shin   מהש

Imagine little lights on top of each letter

Interlace the Name of God selected.
In this case, מהש - Mem, Hei, Shin with אהיה - Alef, Hei, Yod, Hei.
It will look like this: אמההישה - Alef, Mem, Hei, Hei, Yod, Shin, Hei.
Pronounce these words.

Now, pronounce these other words:

יאהדונהי - Yod, Alef, Hei, Dalet, Vav, Nun, Hei, Yod.
This interlaces Yahweh and Adonai, activating the Name of God selected.

Do not stress. A complete chart with each of the 72 Names of God, interlaced is provided below.

Visualize the lights joining and coming up through the top of the second Star of David, where they are in. Then, visualize the lights entering into your brain, then into your heart, and then into your liver. Then moving from your liver up to your heart, then to your brain. Then, moving from brain to heart, brain to heart, brain to heart (3 times). Visualize the light exiting your brain and turning into a shower of light all over you. Bring the light into your third eye and project it into the third star, which has the person receiving the blessing, the healing.

Seal the process pronouncing: - אֵל שַׁדַּי 'El Shaddai'.

If you are working with the Names of God for your benefit, then you only need to visualize two Stars of David, instead of three. The treatment here finishes with you enjoying the shower of light all over you, skipping the part of bringing it to your third eye and proyecting it into a third star.

The 72 Names of God - Complete Chart

1. והו - Vav, Hei, Vav. אוההיוה - Alef, Vav, Heh, Hei, Yod, Vav, Hei.
   Clears karma from this and previous lives. Induces repentance.

2. ילי - Yod, Lamed, Yod. איהליה - Alef, Yod, Hei, Lamed, Yod, Yod, Hei.
   Heals fractured soul. Heals psychological disturbances.
   Recovers our Divine Spark.

3. סיט - Samech, Yod, Teit. אסהייטה - Alef, Samech, Hei, Yod, Yod, Teit, Hei.
   Miracles. Creates miracles in all areas of life.

4. עלם - Ayin, Lamed, Mem. אעהלימה - Alef, Ayin, Hei, Lamed, Yod, Mem, Hei.
   Eliminates negative thinking and negative energy.
   Relieves worry, bad temper, temper tantrums.

5. מהש - Mem, Hei, Shin. אמההישה - Alef, Mem, Hei, Heh, Yod, Shin, Hei.
   Heals spirit, mind and body. Also heals negative situations.
   Heals families, businesses.

6. ללה - Lamed, Lamed, Hei. אלהליהה - Alef, Lamed, Hei, Lamed, Yod, Hei, Hei.
   Protection and prophecy during dream state.
   Allows working with any Name of God, at any time.

7. אכא - Alef, Kaf, Alef. אאהכיאה - Alef, Alef, Hei, Kaf, Yod, Alef, Hei.
   Activates our DNA. Brings our life into order.
   Hope and strength when we feel all is Lost.

8. כהת -Kaf, Hei, Tav. אכההיתה - Alef, Kaf, Hei, Hei, Yod, Tav, Hei.
   Removes anxiety, stress and negative energies.
   Fills us with positive energy. Nullifies bad decrees.

9. הזי - Hei, Zain, Yod. אההזייה - Alef, Heh, Hei, Zain, Yod, Yod, Hei.
   Accesses Angelic Network to bring order into our lives.
   Connection with the Positive Angels.

10. אלד - Alef, Lamed, Dalet. אאהלידה - Alef, Alef, Hei, Lamed, Yod, Dalet, Hei.
    Protection from the evil eye, from the negative energy of others.
    Protection from bad dreams.

11. לאו - Lamed, Alef, Vav. אלהאיוה - Alef, Lamed, Hei, Alef, Yod, Vav, Hei.
    Clears places of negative energies.
    Places us in a circle of purified and protective energy.

12. ההע - Heh, Hei, Ain. אהההיעה - Alef, Hei, Hei, Hei, Yod, Ain, Hei.
    Uses the Power of Love to heal ourselves and others.
    Transforms hatred into Love.

13. יזל - Yod, Zain, Lamed. איהזילה Alef, Yod, Hei, Zain, Yod, Lamed, Hei.
    Transformation to achieve Inner Messiah.
    Makes us participant in bringing Heaven on Earth.

14. מבה - Mem, Beit, Heh. אמהביהה - Alef, Mem, Hei, Beit, Yod, Hei, Hei.
    Achieves peaceful solutions to avert conflicts.
    Helps us not to be judgemental towards others.

15. הרי - Hei, Reish, Yod. אההרייה - Alef, Hei, Hei, Reish, Yod, Yod, Hei.
Making right decisions.
Ability to see the consequences of our behaviour and their long-term effects.

16. הקם - Hei Kuf, Mem. אההקימה - Alef, Hei, Hei, Kuf, Yod, Mem, Hei.
Removes depression.
Strength to rise up when feeling down and defeated.

17. לאו - Lamed, Alef, Vav. אלהאיוה - Alef, Lamed, Hei, Alef, Yod, Vav, Hei.
Removes egotism and selfishness, allowing us to live a more spiritual, selfless life.

18. כלי - Kaf, Lamed, Yod. אכהלייה - Alef, Kaf, Hei, Lamed, Yod, Yod, Hei.
Fertility; either for having children, or for being fruitful and successful in our plans and projects.

19. לוו - Lamed, Vav, Vav. אלהויוה - Alef, Lamed, Hei, Vav, Yod, Vav, Hei.
Dialling God. Removes obstacles to our prayers. Our prayers are answered.

20. פהל - Pey, Hei, Lamed. אפההילה - Alef, Pey, Hei, Hei, Yod, Lamed, Hei.
Victory over Addictions.
Spiritual strength.

21. נלך - Num, Lamed, Caf. אנהלידה - Alef, Num, Hei, Lamed, Yod, Caf, Hei.
Strength to persevere till the end, particularly when feeling stuck, paralysed and without energy.

22. ייי - Yod, Yod, Yod. איהייה - Alef, Yod, Hei, Yod, Yod, Yod, Hei.
Priestly blessings for wellness.
Clears away the negative energy of others from our aura field.

23. מלה - Mem, Lamed, Heh. אמהליהה - Alef, Mem, Hei, Lamed, Yod, Hei, Hei.
Creates opportunities to share the Divine Light Force with others.

24. חהו - Cheit, Hei, Vav. אחההווה - Alef, Cheit, Hei, Hei, Yod, Vav, Hei.
Removes jealously, envy and materialism from our hearts.

25. נתה - Nun, Tav, Hei. אנהתיהה - Alef, Nun, Hei, Tav, Yod, Hei, Hei.
Ability to communicate truths in an uplifting manner.
Courage to speak up and to listen up.

26. האא - Hei, Alef, Alef. אההאיאה - Alef, Heh, Hei, Alef, Yod, Alef, Hei.
Brings order to life. Creates order where there is chaos.
Strength to complete projects.

27. ירת - Yod, Reish, Tav. איהריתה - Alef, Yod, Hei, Reish, Yod, Tav, Hei.
Alliance with the Light. Helps us to live freely, purely, and with joy in our hearts.

28. שאה - Shin, Alef, Hei. אשהאיהה - Alef, Shin, Hei, Alef, Yod, Hei, Hei.
Soul Mate. Removes blockages to being with our soul mate.
Strengthens families and friendships.

29. ריי - Reish, Yod, Yod.ארהייה - Alef, Reish, Hei, Yod, Yod, Hei.
Clearing hatred from our heart.
Thus, allowing for a closer connection with the spiritual world.

30. אום - Alef, Vav, Mem. אאהומה - Alef, Alef, Hei, Vav, Yod, Mem, Hei.
Creates bridges between us and other people, and between us and God.

31. לכב - Lamed, Caf, Beit. אלהכיבה - Alef, Lamed, Hei, Caf, Yod, Beit, Hei.
Removes the habit to procrastinate.
Strength to overcome obstacles, and to finish what we started.

32. ושר - Vav, Shin, Reish. אוהשירה - Alef, Vav, Hei, Shin, Yod, Reish, Hei.
Helps us to break cycles of repetitive mistakes, to get unstuck and out of negative situations.

33. יחו - Yod, Cheit, Vav. איהחיוה - Alef, Yod, Hei, Cheit, Yod, Vav, Hei.
Transmutes our dark side into light. Removes self-centredness.

34. להח - Lamed, Hei, Cheit. אלההיחה - Alef, Lamed, Hei, Hei, Yod, Cheit, Hei.
Helps us to let go of stubborn ego, allowing for a greater connection to the Divine Mind.

35. כוק - Caf, Vav, Kuf. אכהויקה - Alef, Caf, Hei, Vav, Yod, Kuf, Hei.
Purifies and sublimizes our sexual energy.
Recollects sparks that were lost due to selfish sexual acts.

36. מנד - Mem, Nun, Dalet. אמהנידה - Alef, Mem, Hei, Nun, Yod, Dalet, Hei.
Eliminates fear from our life, allowing us to live motivated by love and not by fear.

37. אני - Alef, Nun, Yod. אאהנייה - Alef, Alef, Hei, Nun, Yod, Yod, Hei.
Long range vision of our actions. Grasping the big picture behind our obstacles.

38. חעמ - Cheit, Ain, Mem. אחהעימה - Alef, Cheit, Hei, Ain, Yod, Mem, Hei.
Creates a healthy circle of giving and receiving.

39. רהע - Reish, Hei, Ain.ארההיעה - Alef, Reish, Hei, Hei, Yod, Ain, Hei.
Transforms life's hardships into blessings. Helps us to grow through hardships.

40. ייז - Yod, Yod, Zain. איהייזה - Alef, Yod, Hei, Yod, Yod, Zain, Hei.
    Helps us to speak with wisdom, to speak the right words to transform our reality.

41. ההה - Hei, Hei, Hei. אהההיהה - Alef, Hei, Heh, Hei, Yod, Heh, Hei.
    Priestly blessing to bring healing and well-being in all areas of life.
    Induces self-esteem.

42. מיכ - Mem, Yod, Caf. אמהייכה - Alef, Mem, Hei, Yod, Yod, Caf, Hei.
    Connects us to spiritual secrets, reveals the concealed. Promotes telepathy.

43. וול - Vav, Vav, Lamed. אוהוילה - Alef, Vav, Hei, Vav, Yod, Lamed, Hei.
    Sets our spirit free from negative forces. Gives us control over our destiny.

44. ילה - Yod, Lamed, Hei. איהליה - Alef, Yod, Hei, Lamed, Yod, Heh, Hei.
    Sweetens and removes judgements against us. Helps to prevent a harsh fate.

45. סאל - Samech, Alef, Lamed. אסהאילה - Alef, Samech, Hei, Alef, Yod, Lamed, Hei.
    Summons the forces of prosperity. Brings good fortune, wealth and abundance.

46. ערי - Ain, Reish, Yod. אעהרייה - Alef, Ain, Hei, Reish, Yod, Yod, Hei.
    Brings in the power of faith. Certainty that we will get everything we need.

47. עשל - Ain, Shin, Lamed. אעהשילה - Alef, Ain, Hei, Shin, Yod, Lamed, Hei.
    Resolves internal conflicts. Removes blockages from our life.

48. מיה - Mem, Yod, Hei. אמהיהה - Alef, Mem, Hei, Yod, Hei, Hei.
    Encourages unity, sensitivity, respect, tolerance and closeness among people.

49. והו - Vav, Hei, Vav. אוההיוה - Alef, Vav, Hei, Hei, Yod, Vav, Hei.
    Happiness and Gratitude. Brings joy, optimism, and life appreciation.

50. דני - Dalet, Nun, Yod. אדהנייה - Alef, Dalet, Hei, Nun, Yod, Yod, Hei.
    Prophecy. Awakens spiritual growth. Confidence that everything is possible.

51. החש - Hei, Cheit, Shin. אהההישה - Alef, Hei, Hei, Cheit, Yod, Shin, Hei.
    Forgiveness of our sins. Power of repentance to repair past sins.

52. עמם - Ain, Mem, Mem. אעהמימה - Alef, Ain, Hei, Mem, Yod, Mem, Hei.
    Connects us with the Creator and the secrets from heaven. Passion.

53. ננא - Nun, Nun, Alef. אנהניאה - Alef, Nun, Hei, Nun, Yod, Alef, Hei.
    Strong spiritual protection by Archangel Michael.

54. נית - Nun, Yod, Tav. אנהיתה - Alef, Nun, Hei, Yod, Yod, Tav, Hei.
Immortality to cancel death. Avoids the death of our projects.

55. מבה - Mem, Beit, Hei. אמהביה - Alef, Mem, Hei, Beit, Yod, Hei, Hei.
Commitment and power to achieve our objectives. Peaceful solution to conflict.

56. פוי - Peh, Vav, Yod. אפהוייה - Alef, Peh, Hei, Vav, Yod, Yod, Hei.
Helps us to get rid of anger. Removes hostility, and hatred from our hearts.

57. נמם - Nun, Mem, Mem. אנהמימה - Alef, Nun, Hei, Mem, Yod, Mem, Hei.
Power to overcome our limitations. Listening to our soul.

58. ייל - Yod, Yod, Lamed. איהיילה - Alef, Yod, Hei, Yod, Yod, Lamed, Hei.
Getting God to fight our battles.

59. הרח - Hei, Reish, Cheit. אההריחה - Alef, Hei, Hei, Reish, Yod, Cheit, Hei.
Establishes umblilical cord with God. Removes spiritual darkness.

60. מצר - Mem, Tsadi, Reish. אמהצירה - Alef, Mem, Hei, Tsadi, Yod, Reish, Hei.
Delivery from emotional bondage-negative patterns.

61. ומב - Vav, Mem, Beit. אוהמיבה - Alef, Vav, Hei, Mem, Yod, Beit, Hei.
Brings the healing of spiritual water to heal us physically and spiritually.

62. יהה - Yod, Hei, Hei. איההיהה - Alef, Yod, Hei, Hei, Yod, Hei, Hei.
Ability to reach others teaching truths through our life example.
Parent-Teacher not Preacher.

63. ענו - Ain, Nun, Vav. אעהניוה - Alef, Ain, Hei, Nun, Yod, Vav, Hei.
Creates in us appreciation for what we have now.
Helps us to overcome past pains.

64. מחי - Mem, Cheit, Yod. אמההייה - Alef, Mem, Hei, Cheit, Yod, Yod, Hei.
Helps us with self-esteem and to see our inner beauty, and for others to also admire that beauty in us.

65. דמב - Dalet, Mem, Beit. אדהמיבה - Alef, Dalet, Hei, Mem, Yod, Beit, Hei.
Knowing consequences of bad behaviour. Conscience to help and not to judge.

66. מנק - Mem, Nun, Kof. אמהניקה - Alef, Mem, Hei, Nun, Yod, Kof, Hei.
Ability to solve problems in a spiritual way. Eliminates victim's mentality.

67. איע - Alef, Yod, Ain. אאהייעה - Alef, Alef, Hei, Yod, Yod, Ain, Hei.
Power over time. Overcome disappointment from expectations.

68. חבו - Cheit, Beit, Vav. אחהביוה - Alef, Cheit, Hei, Beit, Yod, Vav, Hei.
Contacting departed souls to get advice and support, or to help uplift them to higher realms.

69. ראה - Reish, Alef, Hei.ארהאיהה - Alef, Reish, Hei, Alef, Yod, Hei, Hei.
Wisdom. Blessing to get married. Helps us re-organize our lives.

70. יבמ - Yod, Beit, Mem. איהבימה - Alef, Yod, Hei, Beit, Yod, Mem, Hei.
Removes obstacles to financial success. Success in businesses.

71. היי - Hei, Yod, Yod. אההייה - Alef, Hei, Hei, Yod, Yod, Yod, Hei.
Gifts of prophecy and intuition.
Ability to reach parallel universes of light and abundance.

72. מום - Mem, Vav, Mem. אמהוימה - Alef, Mem, Hei, Vav, Yod, Mem, Hei.
Spiritual cleansing. Helps us learn from our mistakes and correct them.
Improves negotiations.

רחש - Reish, Cheit, Shin. ארהחישה - Alef, Reish, Hei, Cheit, Yod, Shin, Hei
Clears black magic, Clears evil spirits.

דיקרנוסא - Dalet, Yod, Kuf, Reish, Nun, Vav, Samech, Alef - 'DICARNOSA'
Great financial prosperity (pronounce 'DICARNOSA' mentally).

יאהדונהי - Yod, Alef, Hei, Dalet, Vav, Nun, Hei, Yod.
(This interlaces Yahweh and Adonai, activating the Name of God selected)

Reiki Symbols Used in Kabbalah Reiki

Chakana   Cho Ku Rei   Raku

These are the Reiki symbols we will use to perform Kabbalah Reiki:

 Chakana:

The Chakana is the Shamanic Master Symbol. The Chakana carries the essence of creation via Sacred Geometry to do Inca healing. The Chakana is a powerful Energy Tool to clear DNA contaminations, and other contaminations, which could prevent healing to occur.

 Cho Ku Rei:

The Cho Ku Rei is the Reiki Master Symbol. It works as a key. Therefore, we will use it at the beginning and at the end of a treatment. It is used to focus energy. We will use it prior to using the Chakana as a way of saying, we are now focusing the Chakana Power.

 Raku:

The Raku is the completion symbol. It works as a knife and it is used to separate energies. This symbol is used at end of a treatment to cut the connection with the client. This is done, in order to avoid energy drainage from the Reiki practitioner.

Part IV

Special Healing and Advanced Techniques

Special Healing Techniques
How to Release a Person from Black Magic

Open Sacred Space with the following prayers. Pronounce the words in blue, green and purple

בָּרוּךְ אַתָּה יְיָ אֱלֹהֵינוּ מֶלֶךְ הָעוֹלָם   Baruch atah, Adonai, Eloheinu, Melech haolam.
Blessed Are You, Oh Lord, God, King of the Universe

שְׁמַע יִשְׂרָאֵל: יהוה אֱלֹהֵינוּ, יהוה אֶחָד!   Sh'ma Yisrael: Adonai Ehloheinu, Adonai Ehchad! Hear, Oh Israel, The Lord your God, The Lord Is One!

B'sheim Adonai Elohei Yisrael, Mimini Mihael, Miesmoli Gavriel, Milefanai Uriel, Meajorai Rafael, V'al Roshi Shechinat El
In the name of the Lord, the God of Israel, May Michael be at my right hand, Gabriel at my left, Uriel in front of me, Raphael behind me, and all around me the Shekhinah Glory of God

קָדוֹשׁ קָדוֹשׁ קָדוֹשׁ ‑ וַהֲיָה ‑ Vahoyaha. אראריתא ‑ ARARITA. ללה ‑ Lamed, Lamed, Hei לוו ‑ Lamed, Vav, Vav.

Kadosh, Kadosh, Kadosh

Visualize 3 Stars of David: one for you, one for the Names of God and one for your client.

    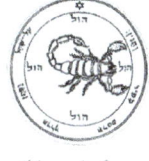

First Seal of The Sun   Fifth Seal of Mars

רחש ‑ Reish, Cheit, Shin ‑ Clears Black Magic, Clears Evil Spirits
ארהחישה ‑ Alef, Reish, Hei, Cheit, Yod, Shin, Hei
יאהדונהי ‑ Yod, Alef, Hei, Dalet, Vav, Nun, Hei, Yod

Letters lid up, join as one, come up from top of 2nd Star, enter 1st Star.
Move brain, heart, liver (3x), then up from top of 1st Star, becomes shower of light.
Concentrates on 3rd Eye, from there send it to person on 3rd Star

 אֵל שַׁדַּי   El Shaddai

Third Seal of Saturn   Third Seal of Jupiter

How to Clear Karma

Open Sacred Space with the following prayers. Pronounce the words in blue, green and purple

בָּרוּךְ אַתָּה יְיָ אֱלֹהֵינוּ מֶלֶךְ הָעוֹלָם   Baruch atah, Adonai, Eloheinu, Melech haolam.
Blessed Are You, Oh Lord, God, King of the Universe

שְׁמַע יִשְׂרָאֵל: יהוה אֱלֹהֵינוּ, יהוה אֶחָד!   Sh'ma Yisrael: Adonai Ehloheinu, Adonai Ehchad! Hear, Oh Israel, The Lord your God, The Lord Is One!

B'sheim Adonai Elohei Yisrael, Mimini Mihael, Miesmoli Gavriel, Milefanai Uriel, Meajorai Rafael, V'al Roshi Shechinat El
In the name of the Lord, the God of Israel, May Michael be at my right hand, Gabriel at my left, Uriel in front of me, Raphael behind me, and all around me the Shekhinah Glory of God

לוו - Lamed, Vav, Vav. ללה - Lamed, Lamed, Hei אראריתא - ARARITA. והיה - Vahoyaha. קדוש קדוש קדוש

Kadosh, Kadosh, Kadosh

Visualize 3 Stars of David: one for you, one for the Names of God and one for your client.

First Seal of The Sun

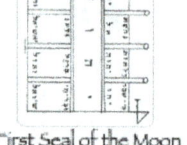
First Seal of the Moon

והו - Vav, Heh, Vav - Clears Karma from this and previous lives
אוהויה - Alef, Vav, Hei, Hei, Yod, Vav, Hei
יאהדונהי - Yod, Alef, Hei, Dalet, Vav, Nun, Hei, Yod
Letters lid up, join as one, come up from top of 2nd Star, enter 1st Star.
Move brain, heart, liver (3x), then up from top of 1st Star, becomes shower of light.
Concentrates on 3rd Eye, from there send it to person on 3rd Star

אֵל שַׁדַּי   El Shaddai

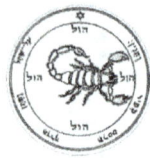
Fifth Seal of Mars

Fifth Seal of Mercury

How to Activate a Person's DNA

Open Sacred Space with the following prayers. Pronounce the words in blue, green and purple

בָּרוּךְ אַתָּה יְיָ אֱלֹהֵינוּ מֶלֶךְ הָעוֹלָם   Baruch atah, Adonai, Eloheinu, Melech haolam.
Blessed Are You, Oh Lord, God, King of the Universe

שְׁמַע יִשְׂרָאֵל: יהוה אֱלֹהֵינוּ, יהוה אֶחָד!   Sh'ma Yisrael: Adonai Ehloheinu, Adonai Ehchad! Hear, Oh Israel, The Lord your God, The Lord Is One!

B'sheim Adonai Elohei Yisrael, Mimini Mihael, Miesmoli Gavriel, Milefanai Uriel, Meajorai Rafael, V'al Roshi Shechinat El
In the name of the Lord, the God of Israel, May Michael be at my right hand, Gabriel at my left, Uriel in front of me, Raphael behind me, and all around me the Shekhinah Glory of God

לוו - Lamed, Vav, Vav.   ללה - Lamed, Lamed, Hei   אראריתא - ARARITA.   וַהֲיָה - Vahoyaha.   קָדוֹשׁ קָדוֹשׁ קָדוֹשׁ

Kadosh, Kadosh, Kadosh

Visualize 3 Stars of David: one for you, one for the Names of God and one for your client.

First Seal of The Sun

Fifth Seal of Jupiter

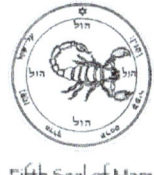
Fifth Seal of Mars

יְלִי - Yod, Lamed, Yod – Activates a Person's DNA
איהלייה - Alef, Yod, Hei, Lamed, Yod, Yod, Hei
יאהדונהי - Yod, Alef, Hei, Dalet, Vav, Nun, Hei, Yod
Letters lid up, join as one, come up from top of 2nd Star, enter 1st Star.
Move brain, heart, liver (3x), then up from top of 1st Star, becomes shower of light.
Concentrates on 3rd Eye, from there send it to person on 3rd Star

אֵל שַׁדַּי   El Shaddai

First Seal of Mars

How to Do a General Healing

Open Sacred Space with the following prayers. Pronounce the words in blue, green and purple

בָּרוּךְ אַתָּה יְיָ אֱלֹהֵינוּ מֶלֶךְ הָעוֹלָם   Baruch atah, Adonai, Eloheinu, Melech haolam.
Blessed Are You, Oh Lord, God, King of the Universe

שְׁמַע יִשְׂרָאֵל: יהוה אֱלֹהֵינוּ, יהוה אֶחָד!   Sh'ma Yisrael: Adonai Ehloheinu, Adonai Ehchad! Hear, Oh Israel, The Lord your God, The Lord Is One!

B'sheim Adonai Elohei Yisrael, Mimini Mihael, Miesmoli Gavriel, Milefanai Uriel, Meajorai Rafael, V'al Roshi Shechinat El
In the name of the Lord, the God of Israel, May Michael be at my right hand, Gabriel at my left, Uriel in front of me, Raphael behind me, and all around me the Shekhinah Glory of God

וָו - Lamed, Vav, Vav. לְלָה - Lamed, Lamed, Hei אראריתא - ARARITA. וַהֲיָה - Vahoyaha. קָדוֹשׁ קָדוֹשׁ קָדוֹשׁ

Kadosh, Kadosh, Kadosh

Visualize 3 Stars of David: one for you, one for the Names of God and one for your client.

First Seal of The Sun

Second Seal of Mars

מהש - Mem, Hei, Shin - Heals Spirit, Mind and Body
אמההישה - Alef, Mem, Hei, Hei, Yod, Shin, Hei
יאהדונהי - Yod, Alef, Hei, Dalet, Vav, Nun, Hei, Yod
Letters lid up, join as one, come up from top of 2nd Star, enter 1st Star.
Move brain, heart, liver (3x), then up from top of 1st Star, becomes shower of light.
Concentrates on 3rd Eye, from there send it to person on 3rd Star

אֵל שַׁדַּי   El Shaddai

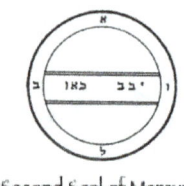
Second Seal of Mercury

Second Seal of Jupiter

How to Do a Healing for Anxiety

Open Sacred Space with the following prayers. Pronounce the words in blue, green and purple

בָּרוּךְ אַתָּה יְיָ אֱלֹהֵינוּ מֶלֶךְ הָעוֹלָם   Baruch atah, Adonai, Eloheinu, Melech haolam.
Blessed Are You, Oh Lord, God, King of the Universe

שְׁמַע יִשְׂרָאֵל: יהוה אֱלֹהֵינוּ, יהוה אֶחָד!   Sh'ma Yisrael: Adonai Ehloheinu, Adonai Ehchad! Hear, Oh Israel, The Lord your God, The Lord Is One!

B'sheim Adonai Elohei Yisrael, Mimini Mihael, Miesmoli Gavriel, Milefanai Uriel, Meajorai Rafael, V'al Roshi Shechinat El
In the name of the Lord, the God of Israel, May Michael be at my right hand, Gabriel at my left, Uriel in front of me, Raphael behind me, and all around me the Shekhinah Glory of God

קָדוֹשׁ קָדוֹשׁ קָדוֹשׁ - Kadosh, Kadosh, Kadosh. וַהֲיָה - Vahoyaha. אראריתא - ARARITA. ללה - Lamed, Lamed, Hei. לוו - Lamed, Vav, Vav.

Visualize 3 Stars of David: one for you, one for the Names of God and one for your client.

First Seal of The Sun

Second Seal of Jupiter

Fifth Seal of Mars

כהת - Kaf, Hei, Tav - Removes Anxiety and Stress
אכההיתה - Alef, Kaf, Hei, Heh, Yod, Tav, Hei
יאהדונהי - Yod, Alef, Hei, Dalet, Vav, Nun, Hei, Yod
Letters lid up, join as one, come up from top of 2nd Star, enter 1st Star.
Move brain, heart, liver (3x), then up from top of 1st Star, becomes shower of light.
Concentrates on 3rd Eye, from there send it to person on 3rd Star

אֵל שַׁדַּי El Shaddai

Second Seal of Mars

How to Do a Healing for Depression

Open Sacred Space with the following prayers. Pronounce the words in blue, green and purple

בָּרוּךְ אַתָּה יְיָ אֱלֹהֵינוּ מֶלֶךְ הָעוֹלָם   Baruch atah, Adonai, Eloheinu, Melech haolam.
Blessed Are You, Oh Lord, God, King of the Universe

שְׁמַע יִשְׂרָאֵל: יהוה אֱלֹהֵינוּ, יהוה אֶחָד!   Sh'ma Yisrael: Adonai Ehloheinu, Adonai Ehchad! Hear, Oh Israel, The Lord your God, The Lord Is One!

B'sheim Adonai Elohei Yisrael, Mimini Mihael, Miesmoli Gavriel, Milefanai Uriel, Meajorai Rafael, V'al Roshi Shechinat El
In the name of the Lord, the God of Israel, May Michael be at my right hand, Gabriel at my left, Uriel in front of me, Raphael behind me, and all around me the Shekhinah Glory of God

לוו - Lamed, Vav, Vav.   ללה - Lamed, Lamed, Hei   אראריתא - ARARITA.   וְהָיָה - Vahoyaha.   קָדוֹשׁ קָדוֹשׁ קָדוֹשׁ
Kadosh, Kadosh, Kadosh

Visualize 3 Stars of David: one for you, one for the Names of God and one for your client.

First Seal of The Sun   Second Seal of Jupiter

הקם - Hei Kuf, Mem - Removes Depression
אההקימה - Alef, Hei, Hei, Kuf, Yod, Mem, Hei
יאהדונהי - Yod, Alef, Hei, Dalet, Vav, Nun, Hei, Yod
Letters lid up, join as one, come up from top of 2nd Star, enter 1st Star.
Move brain, heart, liver (3x), then up from top of 1st Star, becomes shower of light.
Concentrates on 3rd Eye, from there send it to person on 3rd Star

אֵל שַׁדַּי   El Shaddai

Fifth Seal of Mars   Second Seal of Mars

How to Do a Healing for Addictions

Open Sacred Space with the following prayers. Pronounce the words in blue, green and purple

בָּרוּךְ אַתָּה יְיָ אֱלֹהֵינוּ מֶלֶךְ הָעוֹלָם Baruch atah, Adonai, Eloheinu, Melech haolam.
Blessed Are You, Oh Lord, God, King of the Universe

שְׁמַע יִשְׂרָאֵל: יהוה אלהינו, יהוה אחד! Sh'ma Yisrael: Adonai Ehloheinu, Adonai Ehchad! Hear, Oh Israel, The Lord your God, The Lord Is One!

B'sheim Adonai Elohei Yisrael, Mimini Mihael, Miesmoli Gavriel, Milefanai Uriel, Meajorai Rafael, V'al Roshi Shechinat El
In the name of the Lord, the God of Israel, May Michael be at my right hand, Gabriel at my left, Uriel in front of me, Raphael behind me, and all around me the Shekhinah Glory of God

קָדוֹשׁ קָדוֹשׁ קָדוֹשׁ - Lamed, Vav, Vav. לוו - Lamed, Lamed, Hei ללה - אראריתא - ARARITA. וַהֲיָה - Vahoyaha. קָדוֹשׁ קָדוֹשׁ קָדוֹשׁ

Kadosh, Kadosh, Kadosh

Visualize 3 Stars of David: one for you, one for the Names of God and one for your client.

    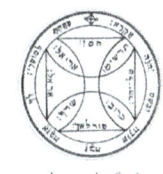

First Seal of The Sun   Seventh Seal of The Sun

פהל - Pey, Hei, Lamed - Victory over Addictions
אפההילה - Alef, Pey, Hei, Heh, Yod, Lamed, Hei
יאהדונהי - Yod, Alef, Hei, Dalet, Vav, Nun, Hei, Yod
Letters lid up, join as one, come up from top of 2nd Star, enter 1st Star.
Move brain, heart, liver (3x), then up from top of 1st Star, becomes shower of light.
Concentrates on 3rd Eye, from there send it to person on 3rd Star

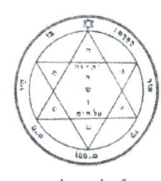

Fifth Seal of Mars

אֵל שַׁדַּי El Shaddai

Second Seal of Mars

How to Call for a Miracle

Open Sacred Space with the following prayers. Pronounce the words in blue, green and purple

בָּרוּךְ אַתָּה יְיָ אֱלֹהֵינוּ מֶלֶךְ הָעוֹלָם   Baruch atah, Adonai, Eloheinu, Melech haolam.
Blessed Are You, Oh Lord, God, King of the Universe

שְׁמַע יִשְׂרָאֵל: יהוה אֱלֹהֵינוּ, יהוה אֶחָד!   Sh'ma Yisrael: Adonai Ehloheinu, Adonai Ehchad! Hear, Oh Israel, The Lord your God, The Lord Is One!

B'sheim Adonai Elohei Yisrael, Mimini Mihael, Miesmoli Gavriel, Milefanai Uriel, Meajorai Rafael, V'al Roshi Shechinat El
In the name of the Lord, the God of Israel, May Michael be at my right hand, Gabriel at my left, Uriel in front of me, Raphael behind me, and all around me the Shekhinah Glory of God

לוו - Lamed, Vav, Vav.   ללה - Lamed, Lamed, Hei   אראריתא - ARARITA.   וההיה - Vahoyaha.   קדוש קדוש קדוש
Kadosh, Kadosh, Kadosh

Visualize 3 Stars of David: one for you, one for the Names of God and one for your client.

First Seal of The Sun

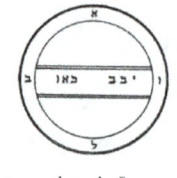
Second Seal of Mercury

Fifth Seal of Mercury

סיט - Samech, Yod, Teit - Miracles. Creates miracles in all areas of life
אסהייטה - Alef, Samech, Hei, Yod, Yod, Teit, Hei
יאהדונהי - Yod, Alef, Hei, Dalet, Vav, Nun, Hei, Yod
Letters lid up, join as one, come up from top of 2nd Star, enter 1st Star.
Move brain, heart, liver (3x), then up from top of 1st Star, becomes shower of light.
Concentrates on 3rd Eye, from there send it to person on 3rd Star

אֵל שַׁדַּי   El Shaddai

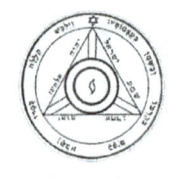
Fourth Seal of Saturn

Soul Retrieval

'Soul Retrieval' refers to reintegrating lost Soul fragments back into a person. Soul Retrieval is a major healing technique in Shamanism. Kabbalah Reiki can also do Soul Retrievals, and with great potency because of the angelic beings involved and the Names of God utilised.

'Soul Loss' happens whenever we suffer a severe physical or emotional trauma. With every traumatic experience, a part of our soul flees the body in order to survive the experience. With every wound our vitality grows weaker, opening the door to several physical and emotional problems.

'Soul Loss' not only affects the individual, but also the people around him. It has the potential of seriously affect relationships. This is because, It plays out when the individual gets emotionally triggered by something that reminds him of the original wound. This mirroring reinforces not only the trauma, but also the beliefs the individual has about himself and the world. This cycle tends to continue, keeping the individual in a prison he feels trapped in, but feels he has no escape from.

What Causes Soul Loss?

- ☐ Any form of abuse, e.g., sexual, emotional, physical, or mental.
- ☐ An event of prolonged grief, pain, and fear, that left one feeling helpless or powerless.
- ☐ An experience of intense rejection or abandonment.
- ☐ A relationship where one loses their personal power.
- ☐ A relationship with a possessive or energy consuming person.
- ☐ The death of a loved one.
- ☐ Major surgery, or near-death experience.
- ☐ Addictions.

Symptoms of a Person Suffering from Soul Loss

- ☐ Feeling incomplete.
- ☐ Chronic depression.
- ☐ Anxiety.
- ☐ Feeling disconnected from the world around.
- ☐ Lack of joy in living.
- ☐ Difficulties making decisions.
- ☐ Loss of energy.
- ☐ Lack of Purpose in Life. Life seems aimless.

How to Do a Kabbalistic Soul Retrieval

Open Sacred Space with the following prayers. Pronounce the words in blue, green and purple:

בָּרוּךְ אַתָּה יְיָ אֱלֹהֵינוּ מֶלֶךְ הָעוֹלָם   Baruch atah, Adonai, Eloheinu, Melech haolam.
Blessed Are You, Oh Lord, God, King of the Universe

שְׁמַע יִשְׂרָאֵל: יהוה אֱלֹהֵינוּ, יהוה אֶחָד!   Sh'ma Yisrael: Adonai Ehloheinu, Adonai Ehchad!
Hear, Oh Israel, The Lord your God,
The Lord Is One!

B'sheim Adonai Elohei Yisrael,
Mimini Mihael, Miesmoli Gavriel, Milefanai Uriel, Meajorai Rafael,
V'al Roshi Shechinat El

In the name of the Lord, the God of Israel,
May Michael be at my right hand, Gabriel at my left, Uriel in front of me, Raphael behind me,
and all around me the Shekhinah Glory of God

לוו - Lamed, Vav, Vav.   ללה - Lamed, Lamed, Hei   אראריתא - ARARITA.   וַהֹיָה - Vahoyaha.   קָדוֹשׁ קָדוֹשׁ קָדוֹשׁ - Kadosh, Kadosh, Kadosh

Visualize 3 Stars of David: one for you, one for the Names of God and one for your client.

First Seal of The Sun

Second Seal of Mars

ילי - Yod, Lamed, Yod - Heals a Fractured Soul
איהליה - Alef, Yod, Hei, Lamed, Yod, Yod, Hei
יאהדונהי - Yod, Alef, Hei, Dalet, Vav, Nun, Hei, Yod

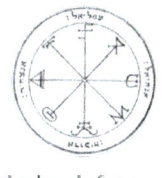
Third Seal of Saturn

Letters lid up, join as one, come up from top of 2nd Star, enter 1st Star.
Move brain, heart, liver (3x), then up from top of 1st Star,
becomes shower of light.
Concentrates on 3rd Eye, from there send it to person on 3rd Star

Third Seal of Jupiter

אֵל שַׁדַּי   El Shaddai

How to Do a Kabbalistic-Shamanic Soul Retrieval

Before Your Client Arrives:

1. Clear and sanctify the space where you are going to perform the healing, with Sage or Palo Santo.
2. Play some Drumming or Shamanic Music on the background.

Starting Session:

3. Greet your client, making him feel welcomed into your sacred space.
4. Ask client if there is anything they would like you to know or consider for the treatment.
5. Ask the client's permission to put your hands on their shoulders briefly to form a connection between the two of you. Also, to touch their body if guided to so, and to place crystals and oils on them (if you intend to do so).
6. Ask your client to take his shoes off, and to lay down on the Reiki Bed.
7. Make sure you have some pillows on the Reiki Bed, both for the head, and for under the knees.
8. Offer your client the choice of having a pillow under his legs for extra comfort.
9. Offer to cover your client with a sheet or blanket.
10. Ask client to relax, to take three deep breaths, and to close his eyes.

Open Sacred Space:

11. Rub your hands with Agua de Ruda (spiritual disinfectant). Put on your spiritual gloves.
12. Open Sacred Space with the following prayers. Pronounce the words in blue, green and purple:

בָּרוּךְ אַתָּה יְיָ אֱלֹהֵינוּ מֶלֶךְ הָעוֹלָם Baruch atah, Adonai, Eloheinu, Melech haolam.

Blessed Are You, Oh Lord, God, King of the Universe

שְׁמַע יִשְׂרָאֵל: יהוה אֱלֹהֵינוּ, יהוה אֶחָד! Sh'ma Yisrael: Adonai Ehloheinu, Adonai Ehchad!
Hear, Oh Israel, The Lord your God, The Lord Is One!

B'sheim Adonai Elohei Yisrael, Mimini Mihael, Miesmoli Gavriel, Milefanai Uriel, Meajorai Rafael, V'al Roshi Shechinat El.

In the name of the Creator God, may Michael be at my right hand, Gabriel at my left, Uriel in front of me, Raphael behind me and all around me God's Shekhinah

13. Call your angelic team: 'I call the Messiah, Archangels Metatron, Sandalphon, Michael, Gabriel, Uriel and Raphael to support me in this journey'.

14. Call the spirit animals, representing the four core principles of life: 'I call the Eagle, the Jaguar, the Hummingbird, the Snake to support me in this journey'.

15. Call upon the Four Elements to assist you in your journey: 'I call upon Fire, Water, Earth, and Air to support me in this journey'.

16. Call upon your Spirit Animals and Soul Hunting Guides: 'I call upon my Spirit Animals and Soul Hunting Guides to support me in this journey'.

17. Place your hands on the shoulders of the client to form connection.

18. Place crystals on each of your client's chakras to help balance his chakras.

19. Take your pendulum and clear your client's chakras, align them, fill them with Divine love and light, and make them of the correct size (move down starting from the Crown Chakra).

Meditation Journey:

20. Visualize you are in a forest, going down towards a beautiful waterfall. There is a cave behind the waterfall. There is an entrance to the cave from the side of the waterfall. The circle in the middle of the Chakana starts to spin clockwise, producing an entrance.

21. Draw the Cho Ku Rei and the Chakana over the entrance to the cave to <u>open</u> the door into the Shamanic worlds.

22. The circle in the middle of the Chakana starts to spin clockwise, producing an entrance for you.

23. Enter into the cave. You are now starting your journey into the Lower World.

24. Turn around towards the door and draw the Cho Ku Rei and the Shin in front of the entrance to the cave to close the door after you and your spiritual friends accompanying you in this journey.

25. Ask to see any other Angelic or Spirit Beings who can help you with wisdom and advise for the healing of your client. Follow your Spirit Beings to where you need to go. They may take you to the Lower World, the Middle World, or the Upper World. Most of the time they will take you to the top layer of the Lower World. Listen to the messages that the Angelic or Spirit Beings that come to you tell you. Thank them for their insights.

Soul Retrieval:

26. Follow your Angelic or Soul Hunting Guides to where the Soul Fragments are. They may take you to the Lower World, the Middle World, or the Upper World. Most of the time they will take you to the top layer of the Lower World. You will need to use your mind's eye to visualize this process.

27. The Soul Fragments may look like adults, but they may also look like small children. Sometimes they appear hiding, either inside the trunk of a tree, trapped on a tree, or sitting by a river shore.

28. Talk to the Soul Fragments, explain that you are their rescuing team and explain the importance of their returning and reintegrating to their person for the benefit of person as a whole. Most of the time, the Soul Fragment will accept to return immediately. Should they place resistance, get your Power Animals to offer their wisdom to the Soul Fragment until they feel ready to return.

29. Sometimes, the Soul Fragments are held hostage by negative entities. If so, ask the negative entities to release the soul fragments. If the entities offer resistance, ask them to release it in the name of Mother and Father Divine.

30. Imagine holding the Soul Fragments in your hands and take them back home.

31. Journey back to the entrance of the cave.

32. Draw the Cho Ku Rei and the Chakana and <u>exit</u> through the circle inside the Chakana.

33. Draw the Cho Ku Rei and the ש Shin and over the entrance to the cave to <u>close</u> the door.

34. Now that you are outside the lower world walk towards your client.

35. Now, you are present with your client and will begin the reintegration of the Lost Soul Fragments into your client. Cup your hands, in the shape of a circle. Move them in the direction of your client's crown chakra and gently blow through it saying: 'I now give to you everything that belongs to you, and I keep nothing'.

36. Pronounce the words in blue and green:

לוו - Lamed, Vav, Vav. ללה - Lamed, Lamed, Hei אראריתא - ARARITA - וַהֲיָה Vahoyaha. קָדוֹשׁ קָדוֹשׁ קָדוֹשׁ
Kadosh, Kadosh, Kadosh

Visualize 3 Stars of David: one for you, one for the Names of God and one for your client.

First Seal of The Sun

Second Seal of Mars

ילי - Yod, Lamed, Yod - Heals a Fractured Soul
איהליה - Alef, Yod, Hei, Lamed, Yod, Hei
יאהדונהי - Yod, Alef, Hei, Dalet, Vav, Nun, Hei, Yod

Letters lid up, join as one, come up from top of 2nd Star, enter 1st Star.
Move brain, heart, liver (3x), then up from top of 1st Star, becomes shower of light.
Concentrates on 3rd Eye, from there send it to person on 3rd Star

אֵל שַׁדַּי El Shaddai

Third Seal of Saturn

Third Seal of Jupiter

37. Wave your hands around your client's body, enveloping him in a cloud of love and light.

38. Swipe your right hand over your client, from head to toe, as a way of closing the healing.

39. Draw the Cho Ku Rei ☯ over your client.

40. Draw the Raku ϟ to cut the connection with your client.

41. Apply Colonia de Ruda on your hands to spiritually sanitize them and remove your spiritual gloves, place them in a spiritual backet of fire for purification (visualize this process).

<u>Close Sacred Space:</u>

42. Thank your Angelic team, Totem Animals, your Power Animals, your Soul Hunting Guides, and the spirit animals representing the four core principles of life: 'I thank my Totem Animals, my Power Animals and the Eagle, the Jaguar, the Hummingbird, and the Snake for assisting me during this journey'.

43. Ask your client how he felt and for any impressions or messages he may have received.

44. Debrief with your client on the advice and wisdom that your received for him.

45. After your client leaves, cleanse the room and yourself with either Sage or Palo Santo.

Giving a Kabbalah Reiki Treatment - Step by Step

Clear and sanctify the space where you are going to perform the healing, with palo santo. Play some Angelic on the background.

Greet your client, making him feel welcomed. Ask client if there is anything they would like you to consider for the treatment.

Ask the client's permission to place crystals and oils on them (if you intend to do so).

Ask your client to take their shoes off, lay down on the Reiki Bed. Ask client to take three deep breaths, and to close his eyes.

Open Sacred Space with the following prayers. Pronounce the words in blue, green and purple:

בָּרוּךְ אַתָּה יְיָ אֱלֹהֵינוּ מֶלֶךְ הָעוֹלָם   Baruch atah, Adonai, Eloheinu, Melech haolam. Blessed Are You, Oh Lord, God, King of the Universe

שְׁמַע יִשְׂרָאֵל: יהוה אֱלֹהֵינוּ, יהוה אֶחָד!   Sh'ma Yisrael: Adonai Ehloheinu, Adonai Ehchad! Hear, Oh Israel, The Lord your God, The Lord Is One!

B'sheim Adonai Elohei Yisrael, Mimini Mihael, Miesmoli Gavriel, Milefanai Uriel, Meajorai Rafael, V'al Roshi Shechinat El.
In the name of the Creator God, may Michael be at my right hand, Gabriel at my left, Uriel in front of me, Raphael behind me and all around me God's Shekhinah.

Call your angelic team: 'I call the Messiah, Archangels Metatron, Sandalphon, Michael, Gabriel, Uriel and Raphael to be with now'.

Clear and balance the chakras with the pendulum. Anticlockwise to clear. Then, clockwise to align and fill with Divine love and light. From crown to root chakra.

Place crystals on each of the chakras (optional).

Pronounce the words in blue and green:

לוו Lamed, Vav, Vav.   ללה Lamed, Lamed, Hei   אראריתא - ARARITA Vahoyaha.   וַהֲיָה קָדוֹשׁ קָדוֹשׁ קָדוֹשׁ Kadosh, Kadosh, Kadosh

Visualize 3 Stars of David: one for you, one for the Names of God and one for your client.
The next two lines apply to Mem, Hei, Shin, the Name for Healing. This is as an example
You may replace it with the Name of your choice

First Seal of The Sun

Second Seal of Mars

מהש - Mem, Hei, Shin - Heals Spirit, Mind and Body
אמההישה - Alef, Mem, Hei, Hei, Yod, Shin, Hei
יאהדונהי - Yod, Alef, Hei, Dalet, Vav, Nun, Hei, Yod

Third Seal of Saturn

Letters lid up, join as one, come up from top of 2nd Star, enter 1st Star. Move brain, heart, liver (3x), then up from top of 1st Star, becomes shower of light. Concentrates on 3rd Eye, from there send it to person on 3rd Star
El Shaddai   אֵל שַׁדַּי

Third Seal of Jupiter

Do the Raku Symbol in order to cut the connection.
Close Sacred Space by thanking your angelic friends, who helped you during this healing.
Debrief with your client on what your received for him during the healing. Ask your client for any impressions they may have received.
After the session, cleanse the room and yourself with palo santo.

Ana Bekoach
The 42-letter Name of God

The Ana Bekoach, or the 42-letter Name of God, is an extremely powerful prayer. It is the code that was used on Creation. When reciting the Ana Bekoach, we enrich our lives with pure spiritual light.

    The Ana b'Koach contains the 42-letter name of God, concealed in the first letter of each word in the prayer.
The 42 words of Ana b'Koach are split into seven verses of six words each, and the first letter of each of the six words of each line are combined to form one six-letter Divine name, each of which forms aspects or attributes of the 42-letter name.

צְרוּרָה	תַּתִּיר	יְמִינְךָ	גְּדוּלַּת	בְּכֹחַ	אָנָּא
tzerurah	tatir	yeminecha	g'dulat	b'koach	ana
נוֹרָא	טַהֲרֵנוּ	שַׂגְּבֵנוּ	עַמְּךָ	רִנַּת	קַבֵּל
nora	taharenu	sagvenu	amecha	rinat	kabel
שָׁמְרֵם	כְּבָבַת	יִחוּדְךָ	דּוֹרְשֵׁי	גִּבּוֹר	נָא
shamrem	k'vavat	yichudecha	dorshei	gibor	na
גָּמְלֵם	תָּמִיד	צִדְקָתְךָ	רַחֲמֵי	טַהֲרֵם	בָּרְכֵם
gamlem	tamid	tzidkatecha	rachamei	taharem	barchem
עֲדָתְךָ	נַהֵל	טוּבְךָ	בְּרֹב	קָדוֹשׁ	חֲסִין
adatecha	nahel	tuvcha	b'rov	kadosh	chasin
קְדֻשָּׁתְךָ	זוֹכְרֵי	פְּנֵה	לְעַמְּךָ	גֵּאֶה	יָחִיד
kdushatecha	zochrei	p'neh	l'am'ach	ge'eh	yachid
תַּעֲלוּמוֹת	יוֹדֵעַ	צַעֲקָתֵנוּ	וּשְׁמַע	קַבֵּל	שַׁוְעָתֵנוּ
ta'alumot	yodeh	tza'akatenu	ush'ma	kabel	sha'vatenu

וָעֶד:	לְעוֹלָם	מַלְכוּתוֹ,	כְּבוֹד	שֵׁם	בָּרוּךְ	(בלחש)
va'ed	le'olam	malchuto	kevod	shem	baruch	(silently)

Ana B'koach

Ana B'koach g'dulat yeminecha tatir tzerurah
kabel rinat amecha sagvenu taharenu nora
na gibor dorshei yichudecha k'vavat shamrem
barchem taharem rachamei tzidkatecha tamid gamlem

Chasin kadosh b'rov tuvcha nahel adatecha
yachid ge'eh l'am'ach p'neh zochrei kdushatecha
sha'vatenu kabel ush'ma tza'akatenu yodeh ta'alumot
baruch shem kevod malchuto le'olam va'ed.

Oh God, by the great power of your right hand, please set the captives free;
Oh, Mighty One, accept the prayer of your people, strengthen us, cleanse us.
Almighty God, guard us, those who seek You, as the apple of your eye;
Bless us, cleans us, have mercy of us, grant us your truth.

Oh, Mighty and Holy God, by your abundant grace, guide your people,
Oh, Unique and Exalted One, remember your people, those who remember your holiness.
You who know all secret thoughts, accept our prayer, hear our cry.
Blessed be the Name of Your glorious majesty forever and ever.

> ▶ YouTube Ana B'Ko'ach (A Kabbalistic Prayer) (2 Versions - Music & Acapella) (Lila Sakura)

Pitum HaKetoret - The Blending of the Incense

The person who says, reads or scans the Pitum HaKetoret is protected from all kinds of danger and evil, including, witchcraft, plagues,
diseases, negative judgements, and death, as the powers of darkness do not have power over such a person.

Reading the Pitum Ha Ketoret brings us closer to God, as it has the power to break Klipot (energetic shells that separate us from the
Light of God).

The Pitum Ha Ketoret opens the channels of success, bringing us wealth, sustenance, good fortune and abundant wealth.

'If people would understand the importance and value of this text, they would make it as a golden crown over their heads' (Rashbi).

Pitum Ha Ketoret
(Hebrew)

Ata hu Adonai Eloheinu Shehk'tiro Avotainu lefanecha et ketoret hasamim b'zman sheh Beit HaMikdash kayam k'asher tzevita otam al yad Moshe neviyach kakatuv b'Torahtach. Vayomer Adonai el Moshe kach lecha samim nataf, ushchelet, vechelbunah samim ulevonah zakah bahd bevahd yehiyeh; v'asitah otah ketoret rokach maaseh rokeach memulach tahor kodesh: veshachaktah mimenah hadek venasata mimenah lifnei haehdute b'ohel moed asher iva-eid lechah shama kodesh kodashim tehiyeh lachem: veneh-emar: vehiktir alav Aharon ketoret samim baboker baboker behetivo et hanerot yaktirenah: uvehlot Aharon et hanerot ben ha-arbayim yaktirenah ketoret tamid lifney Adonai ledoroteichemn.

Tanu Rabbanan: Pitum Haketoret Keytzad, Shlosh meot v'shishim ushmonah manim hoyu va. Shlosh meot V'shishim ushmonah manim hayu va shlosh meot v'shishim v'chamisha keminyan yemot hachama maneh b'chol yom. Machatzito baboker umachatziso b'erev. Ushlosha manim yeterim shemehem machnes Kohem Gadol venotel mehem melo chofnav beYom HaKippurim.

Machaziran lamachteshet b'rev Yom HaKippurim kdei lekayem mitzvas daka min hadakah v'chad asar samanim hayu bah v'eilu hen:
(1) Hatzari (2) V'hatziporen (3) V'hachelbenah (4) V'halevonah. Mishkal shiviim shiviim maneh (5) Mor (6) Uktziyah (7) V'shibolet nered (8) V'charkom. Mishkal shisha asar shisha asar manah (9) Kost shneim asar (10) Kilufa shlosha (11) Kinamon tisha.
Borit karshina tishah kabin yeyin kafrisin s'ein telat v'kabin telatah. V'im lo matzah yayin kafrishin mevie chamar cheyvar atik melach sedomit rovah ma'aleh ashan kol shehu.

Rabbi Nosson HaBavli omer af kipat hayarden kol-shehe im natan ba dvash pesalah v'im chiser achat mikol samamnneyah chayav mitah. Raban Shimon ben Gamliel omer: hatzori eino eilah sheraf hanotef m'atzei hakataf. Borit karshinah lemah he va-ah kdei l'shapot bah et hatziporen kdei shetehey na-ah. Yayin kafrisin lemah hu vah kdei lishrot bo et hatziporen kdei shetehey azah. V'halo mi raglayim yafin la eilah sh'ein machnisin mei raglayim baMikdash mipnei hakavod. Tanya Rabbi Nasat omer: K'shu shochek omer Hadek Heytev. Heytev Hadek mifnei shehakol yafeh labesamim. Pitmah lachatzain kesherah. L'shalish u'leraviya lo shamanu. Amar Rabbi Yehuda: zeh haklal: im kemidata keshera lachatzain, v'im chiser achat mikol samamneyah chayav mita.

Taney var kappara: Achat l'shishim oh l'shviim shanah haytah va-ah shel shiraim lachatzain. Veod taney Bar Kappara: ilu haya noten ba kortov shel dvash ein adam yachol laamod mipnei reichah. Velamah ein me'arvin bah dvash mipney she'haTorah amrah: ki chol seor v'chol dvash lo taktiru mimenu isheh l'Adonai. Adonai tziva-os imanu misgav lanu Elohey Yaakov selah. Adonai tzavaos ashrei adam boteach bach. Adonai hoshiyah. HaMelech yaneinu veyom kareinu. V'arvah l'Adonai minchas Yehuda v'Yerushalayim. Kimey olam uchshanim kadmoniyos.

 Pitum haKetoret + transliteration + english translation (Mahdiya Dijkhof)

The Blending of the Incense - Pitum HaKetoret
(English)

You are Adonai, our God, before whom our Forefathers placed the sweet incense at the time the Holy Temple stood as You commanded them by Moses Your prophet as it written in Your Torah. And God said to Moses, take for yourself spices: stacte, onyche, and galbanum sweet spices and pure frankincense each will be of equal weight and make it ot incence a pharmacist's work purified by salt and pulverized thoroughly and you should place it before the testimony in the Tent of Meeting where I will meet with You Holy of Holies will it be for you. It is also said upon it, Aharon shall place the incense spices every morning when he cleans the Menorah lamps. He will place it and when Aharon lights the lamps in the afternoon, he places the incense always before Adonai throughout the generations.

The Pitum HaKetoret (The Blending of the Incense)
Our sages taught: how to prepare the incense 368 portions were contained therein 365 like the days of the solar year,
1 portion of each day half in the morning and half in the evening and
3 extra portions from which the High Priest took and render 2 fistfuls on Yom Kippur
he would return them to the mortar on the mortar on the eve of Yom Kippur in order to fulfill the mitzvah to make it finer than fine.

Eleven kinds of spices were in it and they are:
(1) Balsam (2) Onycha (3) Galbanum (4) Frankincense weighing 70 portions each (5) Myrrh (6) Cassia (7) Spikenard (8) Saffron, the weight of 16 portions each (9) 12 portions of costus (10) 3 portions of aromatic bark (11) 9 portions of cinnamon. Carshina soap, 9 measurements Cypriote wine, 3 measurements and 3 measurements ('kaab') and if one cannot find Cypriote wine, he should bring old white wine and a quarter of Sodomite salt and a small measure of a smoke-raising herb. Rabbi Natan HaBavli also says a small amount of plant from the Jordan if one adds honey, it is unfit, and if one omits any of the spices, he is liable to the death penalty.

Rabban Shimon ben Gamliel says, balsam is only the sap that drips from balsam trees. Carshina soap serves what purpose? In order to soak the onycha in it so that the scent will be strong. Although urine is more suitable for it, we do not bring urine into the Temple out of respect. We were taught: Rabbi Natan says when he (the Kohen) grinds he says "Hadek Heytev' 'Heytev HaDek' because the voice is beneficial to the spices if half the quantity is prepared, it is acceptable. A third or a quarter, we have not heard. Rabbi Yehuda said this is the rule regarding the same proportions, half is acceptable, but if he left out any of its spices, he is liable to the death penalty.

We were taught: The Bar Kappara says, once in 60 or 70 years the accummulated leftovers came to half and also, Bar Kappara taught, if one puts it into a kortov of honey, no man would be able to withstand its aroma. So why is the honey not mixed into it? Because the Torah said no veaven nor any honey shall you burn as a fire offering to God. Our Lord of heavenly armies is with us. A stronghold for us is the God of Jacob. Lord of heavenly armies blessed is the man who trusts in You. God save us!
Our King, answer us on the day we call out to You may it please Adonai.
The offering of Judah and Jerusalem, as in the past, and in bygone years.

The Aaronic Blessing

The Aaronic Blessing, also called the Priestly Blessing, is a beautiful blessing that God instructed Aaron and his sons to say over His people (Numbers 6:24–26). Saying this prayer over our client, at the end of a session, is the most beautiful way to finish a Kabbalah Reiki Healing.

יְבָרֶכְךָ יהוה וְיִשְׁמְרֶךָ. יָאֵר יְיָ פָּנָיו אֵלֶיךָ וִיחֻנֶּךָּ. יִשָּׂא יהוה פָּנָיו אֵלֶיךָ, וְיָשֵׂם לְךָ שָׁלוֹם.

Y'va-reh-ch'cha Adonai v'yish-m'reh-cha,
Ya-ayr Adonai pan-ahv ay-le-cha v'yi-chu-neh-cha,
Yi-sa Adonai pan-ahv ay-ley-cha v'ya-sem l'cha shalom.

The Lord bless you and keep you.
The Lord make His face to shine upon you and be gracious unto you.
The Lord lift up His countenance upon you and give you peace

▶ YouTube   Aaronic Blessing in Hebrew
            (lechemtube)

Example of a Healing Session

Baruch atah, Adonai, Eloheinu, Melech haolam. Blessed Are You, Oh Lord, God, King of the Universe

Sh'ma Yisrael: Adonai Ehloheinu, Adonai Ehchad! Baruch shem k'vod malchuto l'olam vaed!
Hear, Oh Israel, The Lord your God, The Lord Is One! Blessed is God's glorious majesty forever and ever!

B'sheim Adonai Elohei Yisrael, Mimini Mihael, Miesmoli Gavriel, Milefanai Uriel, Meajorai Rafael, V'al Roshi Shechinat El
In the name of the Lord, the God of Israel, May Michael be at my right hand, Gabriel at my left, Uriel in front of me,
Raphael behind me, and all around me the Shekhinah Glory of God

I request the presence of Meshiah, Archeangels Metatron, Sandalphon, and all the Archangels of the Tree of Life to be present. Amen.

קָדוֹשׁ קָדוֹשׁ - לוו - Lamed, Vav, Vav. ללה - Lamed, Lamed, Hei אראריתא - ARARITA. וַהֲיָה - Vahoyaha. קָדוֹשׁ - Kadosh, Kadosh, Kadosh.

רחש - Reish, Cheit, Shin. ארהחישה - Alef, Reish, Hei, Cheit, Yod, Shin, Hei - Clears black magic, Clears evil spirits.
1. והו - Vav, Hei, Vav. אוההיוה - Alef, Vav, Hei, Hei, Yod, Vav, Hei. Clears karma from this and previous lives. Induces repentance.
59. הרח - Hei, Reish, Cheit. אההריחה - Alef, Hei, Hei, Reish, Yod, Cheit, Hei. Establishes umblilical cord with God.
58. ייל - Yod, Yod, Lamed. איהילה - Alef, Yod, Hei, Yod, Yod, Lamed, Hei. Getting God to fight our battles.
2. ילי - Yod, Lamed, Yod. איהליה - Alef, Yod, Hei, Lamed, Yod, Yod, Hei. Heals fractured soul. Recovers our Divine Spark.
5. מהש - Mem, Hei, Shin. אמההישה - Alef, Mem, Hei, Hei, Yod, Shin, Hei. Heals spirit, mind and body. Heals families, businesses.
12. ההע - Hei, Hei, Ain. אהההיעה - Alef, Hei, Hei, Hei, Yod, Ain, Hei. Uses the Power of Love to heal ourselves and others.
8. כהת - Kaf, Hei, Tav. אכההיתה - Alef, Kaf, Hei, Hei, Yod, Tav, Hei. Removes anxiety, stress and negative energies.
16. הקם - Hei Kuf, Mem. אההקימה - Alef, Hei, Hei, Kuf, Yod, Mem, Hei. Removes depression. Strength to rise up when feeling down.
36. מנד - Mem, Nun, Dalet. אמהנידה - Alef, Mem, Hei, Nun, Yod, Dalet, Hei. Eliminates fear. Live motivated by love and not fear.
7. אכא - Alef, Kaf, Alef. אאהכיאה - Alef, Alef, Hei, Kaf, Yod, Alef, Hei. Activates our DNA. Brings our life into order.
44. ילה - Yod, Lamed, Hei. איהליהה - Alef, Yod, Hei, Lamed, Yod, Hei, Hei. Sweetens and removes judgements against us.
28. שאה - Shin, Alef, Hei. אשהאיהה - Alef, Shin, Hei, Alef, Yod, Hei, Hei. Soul Mate. Removes blockages to being with our soul mate.
45. סאל - Samech, Alef, Lamed. אסהאילה - Alef, Samech, Hei, Alef, Yod, Lamed, Hei. Summons the forces of prosperity.
3. סיט - Samech, Yod, Teit. אסהייטה - Alef, Samech, Hei, Yod, Yod, Teit, Hei. Miracles. Creates miracles in all areas of life.

יאהדונהי ~ Yod, Alef, Hei, Dalet, Vav, Nun, Hei, Yod
Kadosh, Kadosh, Kadosh

Ana B'koah

Ana b'koach g'dulat yeminecha tatir tzerurah kabel rinat amecha sagvenu taharenu nora na gibor dorshei yichudecha k'vavat shamrembarchem taharem rachamei tzidkatecha tamid gamlem chasin kadosh b'rov tuvcha nahel adatecha yachid ge'eh l'am'ach p'neh zochrei kdushatecha sha'vatenu kabel ush'ma tza'akatenu yodeh ta'alumot baruch shem kevod malchuto le'olam va'ed.

Oh God, by the great power of your right hand, please set the captives free; Oh, Mighty One, accept the prayer of your people, strengthen us, cleanse us. Almighty God, guard us, those who seek You, as the apple of your eye; Bless us, cleans us, have mercy of us, grant us your truth. Oh, Mighty and Holy God, by your abundant grace, guide your people; Oh, Unique and Exalted One, remember your people, those who remember your holiness. You who know all secret thoughts, accept our prayer, hear our cry. Blessed be the Name of Your glorious majesty forever and ever.

Pitum HaKetoret

Ata hu Adonai Eloheinu Shehk'tiro Avotainu lefanecha et ketoret hasamim b'zman s Beit HaMikdash kayam k'asher tzevita otam al yad Moshe neviyach kakatuv b'Torahtach. Vayomer Adonai el Moshe kach lecha samim nataf, ushchelet, vechelbunah samim ulevonah zakah bahd bevahd yehiyeh: v'asitah otah ketoret rokach maaseh rokeach memulach tahor kodesh: veshachaktah mimenah hadek venasata mimenah lifnei haehdute b'ohel moed asher iva-eid lechah shama kodesh kodashim tehiyeh lachem: veneh-emar: vehiktir alav Aharon ketoret samim baboker baboker behetivo et hanerot yaktirenah: uvehlot Aharon et hanerot ben ha-arbayim yaktirenah ketoret tamid lifney Adonai ledoroteichemn.

Tanu Rabbanan: Pitum Haketoret Keytzad, Shlosh meot v'shishim ushmonah manim hoyu va. Shlosh meot V'shishim ushmonah manim hayu va shlosh meot v'shishim v'chamisha keminyan yemot hachama maneh b'chol yom. Machatzito baboker umachatziso b'erev. Ushlosha manim yeterim shemehem machnes Kohem Gadol venotel mehem melo chofnav beYom HaKippurim.

Machaziran lamachteshet b'rev Yom HaKippurim kdei lekayem mitzvas daka min hadakah v'chad asar samanim hayu bah v'eilu hen: (1) Hatzari (2) V'hatziporen (3) V'hachelbenah (4) V'halevonah. Mishkal shiviim shiviim maneh (5) Mor (6) Uktziyah (7) V'shibolet nered (8) V'charkom. Mishkal shisha asar shisha asar manah (9) Kost shneim asar (10) Kilufa shlosha (11) Kinamon tisha. Borit karshina tishah kabin yeyin kafrisin s'ein telat v'kabin telatah V'im lo matzah yayin kafrishin mevie chamar cheyvar atik melach sedomit rovah ma'aleh ashan kol shehu.

Rabbi Nosson HaBavli omer af kipat hayarden kol-shehe im natan ba dvash pesalah v'im chiser achat mikol samamnneyah chayav mitah. Raban Shimon ben Gamliel omer: hatzori eino eilah sheraf hanotef m'atzei hakataf. Borit karshinah Iemah he va-ah kdei l'shapot bah et hatziporen kdei shetehey na-ah. Yayin kafrisin lemah hu vah kdei lishrot bo et hatziporen kdei shetehey azah. V'halo mi raglayim yafin la eilah sh'ein machnisin mei raglayim baMikdash mipnei hakavod. Tanya Rabbi Nasat omer: K'shu shochek omer Hadek Heytev. Heytev Hadek mifnei shehakol yafeh labesamim. Pitmah lachatzain kesherah. L'shalish u'leraviya lo shamanu. Amar Rabbi Yehuda: zeh haklal: im kemidata keshera lachatzain, v'im chiser achat mikol samamneyah chayav mita.

Taney var kappara: Achat l'shishim oh l'shviim shanah haytah va-ah shel shiraim lachatzain. Veod taney Bar Kappara: ilu haya noten ba kortov shel dvash ein adam yachol laamod mipnei reichah. Velamah ein me'arvin bah dvash mipney she'haTorah amrah: ki chol seor v'chol dvash lo taktiru mimenu isheh l'Adonai. Adonai tziva-os imanu misgav lanu Elohey Yaakov selah. Adonai tzavaos ashrei adam boteach bach. Adonai hoshiyah. HaMelech yaneinu veyom kareinu. V'arvah l'Adonai minchas Yehuda v'Yerushalayim. Kimey olam uchshanim kadmoniyos.

The Aaronic Blessing

Y'va-reh-ch'cha Adonai v'yish-m'reh-cha, Ya-ayr Adonai pan-ahv ay-le-cha v'yi-chu-neh-cha,
Yi-sa Adonai pan-ahv ay-ley-cha v'ya-sem l'cha shalom.

The Lord bless you and keep you. The Lord make His face to shine upon you and be gracious unto you. The Lord lift up His countenance upon you and give you peace

Recommended Morning Routine

I would recommend everyone to make a playlist on You Tube, and play it first thing in the morning. Doing so, will enhance victory, protection and high vibrations during the day.

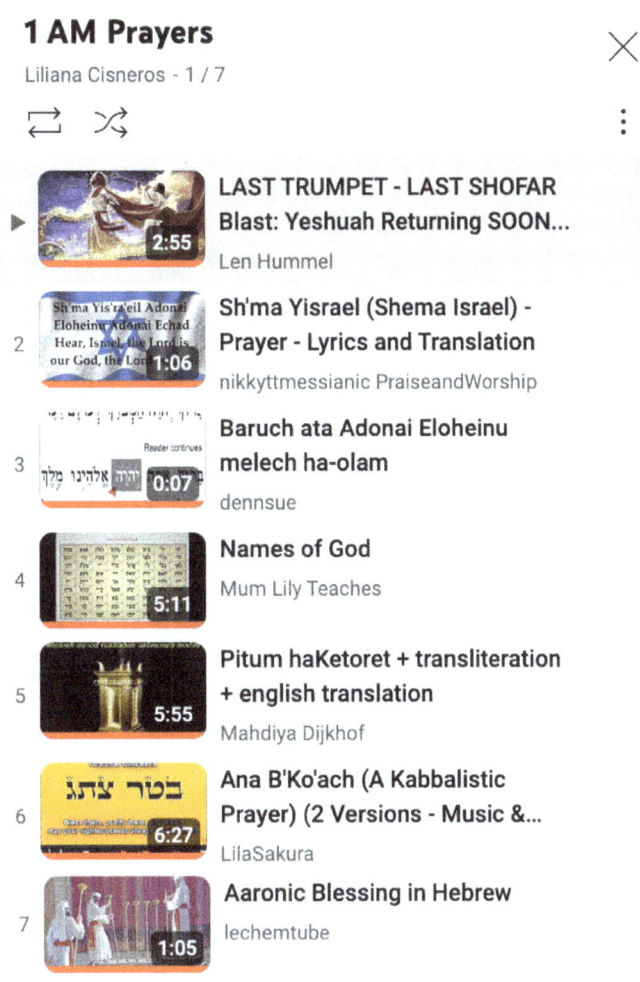

1) Last Trumpet - Last Shofar Blast by Len Hummel

2) Sh'ma Yisrael by nikkyttmessianicPraiseandWorship

3) Baruch ata Adonai by dennsue

4) Names of God by Liliana Cisneros - School of Merkabah

5) Pitum haKetoret by Mahdiya Dijkhof

6) Ana B'Ko'ach (A Kabbalistic Prayer) by LilaSakura

7) Aaronic Blessing in Hebrew by lechemtube

Part V

The Seals of King Solomon

The Seals of King Solomon

Information on King Solomon's Seals is based on 'The Testament of King Solomon', which is an Old Testament apocryphal book. This book deals with Solomon's magical powers over spirits. These seals are known as 'the Kabbalistic Seals' or 'the Kabbalistic Talismans' and they do not resort to the devil or demons.

The things that can be achieved with the Seals of King Solomon may be considered as Miraculous or Magic. The Miraculous or Magic is not something to be afraid of. After all, Magic is science that has not yet been explained. Magic is discovering some of the rules that govern our universe and having the ability to re-create; that is, to change outcomes. Magic is the ability to influence events by using mysterious or supernatural forces. It is taking the control, back into our hands, to re-create our reality. This involves taking action to defy the current laws of nature, in order to bring on a desired change.

Magic has a similarity with Miracles in that, it involves extraordinary changes to situations. We may, at times, participate in Magic or Miracles unaware that we are doing so. It is like we take action intuitively, and this produces a supernatural change of circumstances. The main ingredient for Magic or Miracles is our desire. If our desire for a change is strong enough to bring a supernatural transformation, then that transformation will occur. This can be viewed in cases where people have miraculous healed from various conditions. We may think, when we see this happen, that a person has healed, as it were, by magic. Crystals are wonderful aids to bring on these changes. Like with most things, Magic can be used for good or bad purposes, such us controlling others or causing harm. Use Magic for good purposes only, such as enhancing the quality of life of you and others.

The Seals of King Solomon, also known as the Kabbalistic Seals, are powerful symbols related to King Solomon. King Solomon Seals are used as talismans, or magical symbols in Kabbalah. Each seal has a particular purpose and influences a certain aspect of our life. The powers of the seals are very extensive and are able to perform many wonders.

There are specific ways of working with the seals. However, they are so powerful that simply having them around us, will cause for the seals' energies to radiate all around creating miracles in our life.

The Seals work with the powerful energies of the Sun, the Moon and the Planets in our Solar System.

It is possible to work with the Seals on their own. However, it is also possible to work with them in combination with the 72 Names of God, and even with the Seals of the Archangels. This is the approach that we will be using in Kabbalah Reiki.

The 44 Seals

There are 44 Seals in total. They concern with:
1) The Sun, 2) The Moon, 3) Mars, 4) Jupiter, 5) Mercury, 6) Saturn, and 7) Venus.

1) *The Sun* - Sunday - Gold, Yellow Candle - 7 Seals
The Sun is the giver of life, the luminary of life and self.
These Seals bring magical abilities, protection, honours, riches, prosperity and the esteem of others. They bring favours, benevolence, esteem of others, honours, riches.

2) *The Moon* - Monday - Silver Candle - 6 Seals
The Moon is the nurturer, the luminary of emotions.
These Seals deal with protection from natural disasters, and control over the weather. They bring healing and offer protection while travelling.

3) *Mars* - Tuesday - Red Candle - 7 Seals
Mars is the planet of energy, strength and invulnerability.
These Seals assist with protection, invulnerability, extraordinary strength, vigour, and health. They provide invulnerability, extraordinary strength and vigour.

4) *Mercury* - Wednesday - Orange Candle - 5 Seals
Mercury is the planet of the mind, of communication and knowledge.
These Seals help to attain the impossible, to have harmony with our loved ones, and with eloquence. They help with eloquence and discretion, give knowledge, good memory, and offer solutions through dreams.

5) *Jupiter* - Thursday - Blue (Azure) Candle - 7 Seals
Jupiter is the planet of generosity, prosperity and success.
These Seals bring success, financial abundance, psychic powers, protection, and happiness. They dispel sorrows, panic terrors, bring happiness, and prosperity in business.

6) *Venus* - Friday - Pink, Green Candle - 5 Seals
Venus is the planet of love, attraction, beauty, music and wealth.
These Seals bring love and romance into our lives, enhance personal magnetism, and fruitfulness. They help to extinguish hatred, bring love and talent for music.

7) *Saturn* - Saturday - Black, Blue (midnight) Candle - 7 Seals
Saturn is the planet of order, discipline, authority and processed wisdom.
These Seals bring protection, good luck, success in businesses, and other areas of life. They bring good luck and success in business and negotiations, offers great overall protection.

The Seals of King Solomon - One Page Chart

First Seal of The Sun	Second Seal of The Sun	Third Seal of The Sun	Fourth Seal of The Sun	Fifth Seal of The Sun	Sixth Seal of The Sun	Seventh Seal of The Sun
		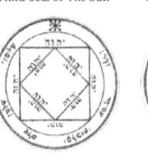	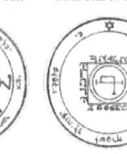			

First Seal of the Moon	Second Seal of the Moon	Third Seal of the Moon	Fourth Seal of the Moon	Fifth Seal of the Moon	Sixth Seal of the Moon
			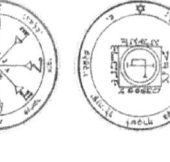		

First Seal of Mars	Second Seal of Mars	Third Seal of Mars	Fourth Seal of Mars	Fifth Seal of Mars	Sixth Seal of Mars	Seventh Seal of Mars
			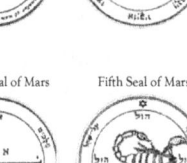			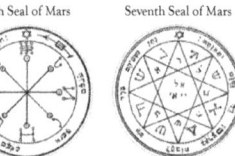

First Seal of Jupiter	Second Seal of Jupiter	Third Seal of Jupiter	Fourth Seal of Jupiter	Fifth Seal of Jupiter	Sixth Seal of Jupiter	Seventh Seal of Jupiter
	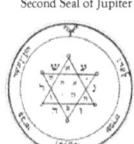			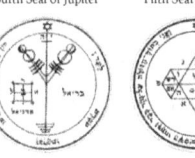	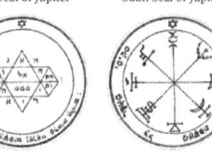	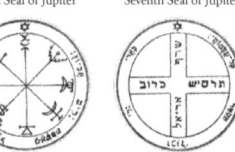

First Seal of Mercury	Second Seal of Mercury	Third Seal of Mercury	Fourth Seal of Mercury	Fifth Seal of Mercury
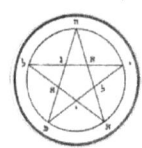	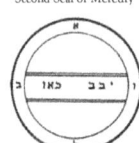		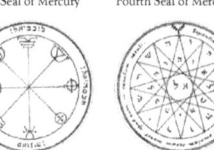	

First Seal of Saturn	Second Seal of Saturn	Third Seal of Saturn	Fourth Seal of Saturn	Fifth Seal of Saturn	Sixth Seal of Saturn	Seventh Seal of Saturn
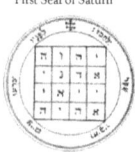	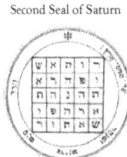			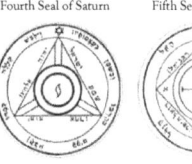	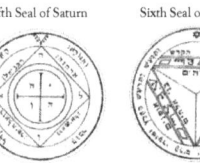	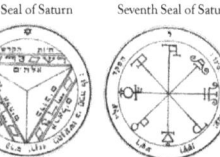

First Seal of Venus	Second Seal of Venus	Third Seal of Venus	Fourth Seal of Venus	Fifth Seal of Venus

The Seals of The Sun

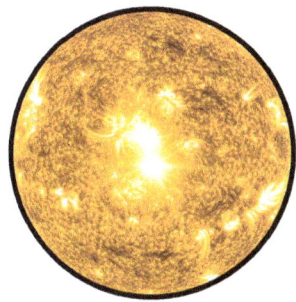

When worn with confidence and reverence, these seals bring magical abilities, supreme protection, honours, riches, prosperity, and the esteem and benevolence of influential people.

Day of Week: Sunday. Perform ritual on a Sunday.
Candle Colour: Gold, Yellow.
Metal It Presides Over: Gold
Number of Seals: 7
The Altar of The Sun: Place the Seal in the middle.
Place a gold or yellow candle on the right side.
Place the incense on the left side. Always face East.

Primary Spirits/Angels Together with Areas of Influence:

1- Metatron – Transformation, Opulence, Magic and Control Over all Beings. Grants all your Wishes.
2- Shemesiel – Material Power and Domination.
3- Rekhodiah – Visions.
4- Melkhiel – Money and Blessings.
5- Paimoniah – Pride and Success.
6- Almiriel – Astral Travel.
7- Dabiel – Invisibility.

These seven pentacle spirits of The Sun can release a tidal wave of cash, riches, treasure, wealth and prosperity into your life. These spirits can also change your luck and bring good fortune from every direction.

These Seven Pentacles/Seals give you:

Seal 1: Magic and Control Over All Beings, including Demons
Seal 2: Makes your Enemies Surrender to You
Seal 3: Fame, Fortune and Fulfilment of Wishes
Seal 4: Lets you See the Spirits at Work
Seal 5: Supernatural Transportability
Seal 6: Power of Invisibility
Seal 7: Release from Addictions

The First Seal of The Sun

Magic and Control Over All Beings, including Angels and Demons, for whatever purpose you wish. Grants all your Wishes. Brings Transformation and Opulence. Will make you shine with Divine Light and get all your desires and wishes fulfilled. Provides protection from any harm or danger.

The Hebrew name of God is 'El Shaddai', meaning: 'The Almighty God, who sustains us and loves us, like a mother loves her child'. The face on this Talisman is of Archangel Metatron. Metatron is the greatest angelic being, who functions as the celestial vice-regent who ministers before The Throne of God. Metatron supervises the celestial liturgy and officiates over the heavenly hosts. Metatron will help you when you perform this ritual.

Instructions

- ☐ Perform ritual on a Sunday, a few minutes before sunrise.
- ☐ Set up an Altar on the East as such: Place the Seal in the middle.
- ☐ Place gold or yellow candle on the right side. Place the incense on the left side.
- ☐ Light the candle.
- ☐ Light the incense.
- ☐ Pick up the seal and hold it.
- ☐ Think, imagine and feel what it is you want.
- ☐ Then, proceed with the following prayers.

Attunement

The Attunement is performed once, that is, the first time you work with the seal

'In the Name of Father and Mother Divine, I receive the attunement to the First Seal of the Sun.'

'The Creator makes my wishes come true'.

Names of God for Attunement

62. Yod.Hei.Hei 23. Mem.Lamed.Hei 19. Lamed.Vav.Vav 70. Yod.Beit.Mem

Leave the talisman on the altar until the candle and incense are extinguished. Then, you are free to wear the Talisman, or use it as you please, such as put it in your pocket, or leave it on the Altar, whatever is most appropriate for you.

Activation

The Activation is performed every time you work with the seal

'In the Names of The Father and Mother Divine, and of the Great King Solomon, I activate the First Seal of The Sun'

'Behold His face and form by whom all things were made and whom all creatures obey'

'Oh, Mighty EL-Shaddai the most powerful God, I ask you to five me control over all beings. Do so by the merit of the great King Solomon.

Sit in silence and feel the power of God coursing through you. Visualize the power coming through the top of your head and out of your hands into the seal. Watch it glow. Place the Talisman down and say:

'In gratitude I come before you EL-Shaddai the great controller of the man and beast. I know that you will grant this request for me through this holy Talisman of the great King Solomon. Amen'

The Seals of the Sun Chart

1st. Seal of The Sun: *Magic and control over all beings. Will make you shine with Divine Light and get all your desires and wishes fulfilled. Provides protection from any harm or danger. The face on this seal is of Archangel Metatron.*

'Behold His face and form by Whom all things were made, and Whom all creatures obey'. 'Oh Mighty EL-Shaddai the most powerful God, I ask you to give me control over all beings. Do so by the merit of the great King Solomon'.

Feel connection with the Seal, then say:

'In gratitude I come before You, El-Shaddai, the great controller of the man and beast. I know that You will grant this wish for me through this holy Talisman of the great King Solomon. Amen'.

Attunement (First Time): 'In the Name of Father and Mother Divine, I receive the attunement to the First Seal of the Sun'. 'The Creator makes my wishes come true'.

Names of God for Attunement: Yod.Hei.Hei (י.ה.ה), Mem.Lamed.Hei (מ.ל.ה), Lamed.Vav.Vav (ל.ו.ו), Yod.Beit.Mem (י.ב.מ)

Activation (After First Time): 'In the Names of Father and Mother Divine, and of the Great King Solomon, I activate the First Seal of the Sun'.

2nd. Seal of The Sun: *Makes your enemies surrender to you. Represses the arrogance and pride of those who stand between you and your aspirations and will make them surrender and fulfill all your requests.*

'I invoke the Angels:
<u>Shemeshiel,</u> who bears the knowledge and power of the Sun.
<u>Paimoniah,</u> who will humble individuals before me.
<u>Rekhodiah,</u> who is very powerful in subjugating individuals to my will.
<u>Malkhiel,</u> who grants blessings, boons and bestows healings.

Feel connection with the Seal.

Attunement (First Time): 'In the Name of Father and Mother Divine, I receive the attunement to the Second Seal of the Sun'. 'The Creator protects me from enemies and evil plans'.

Names of God for Attunement: Cheit.Hei.Vav (ח.ה.ו), Vav.Vav.Lamed (ו.ו.ל), Mem.Tzadi.Reish (מ.צ.ר), Alef.Yod.Ayin (א.י.ע)

Activation (After First Time): 'In the Names of Father and Mother Divine, and of the Great King Solomon, I activate the Second Seal of the Sun'.

3rd. Seal of The Sun: *Fame, fortune and fulfilment of wishes. Empowers you with control and respect, attracts fame and fortune, success and fulfillment of wishes.*

'My Kingdom is an everlasting Kingdom, and my dominion endures from age to age' (Psalm 145: 13). 'Oh Mighty YHVH, the most powerful Name, I ask You to bless me with wealth, more than I will ever need. Do so by the merit of the great King Solomon'.

Feel connection with the Seal, then say:

'In gratitude, I come before You YHVH, the Great Provider. I know that You will grant this request for me through this holy Talisman of the great King Solomon'.

Attunement (First Time): 'In the Name of Father and Mother Divine, I receive the attunement to the Third Seal of the Sun'. 'The Creator helps me to achieve success in my life'.

Names of God for Attunement: Samech.Alef.Lamed (ס.א.ל), Nun.Nun.Alef (נ.נ.א), Ayin.Nun.Vav (ע.נ.ו), Yod.Beit.Mem (י.ב.מ)

Activation (After First Time): 'In the Names of Father and Mother Divine, and of the Great King Solomon, I activate the Third Seal of the Sun'.

4th. Seal of The Sun: *Lets you see the spirits at work. Allows you to look into the soul of another person and see beyond their external impression. This Pentacle aids in enhancing empathy and understanding towards others, while simultaneously diminishing the influence of one's ego.*

'Consider and hear me, O Lord my God; Enlighten my eyes, lest I sleep the sleep of death; lest my eneny say: I have prevailed against him' (Psalm 13: 3,4).

Feel connection with the Seal.

Attunement (First Time): 'In the Name of Father and Mother Divine, I receive the attunement to the Fourth Seal of the Sun'. 'The Creator helps me to channel higher energies'.

Names of God for Attunement: Ayin.Shin.Lamed (ע.ש. ל), Mem.Cheit.Yod (מ.ח.י), Reish.Alef.Hei (ר.א. ה), Nun.Tav.Hei (נ.ת. ה)

Activation (After First Time): 'In the Names of Father and Mother Divine, and of the Great King Solomon, I activate the Fourth Seal of the Sun'.

5th. Seal of The Sun: *Supernatural transportability. Will help you develop mystical powers and open your eyes to foresee the possible dangers from harmful spirits and use their power to your advantage.*

'He shall give His Angels charge over you, to keep you in all your ways. They shall bear you up in their hands' (Psalm 91:11,12).

Feel connection with the Seal, then say:

'In the Names of Father and Mother Divine, and of the Great King Solomon, May my travels be safe and swift. Amen'.

Attunement (First Time): 'In the Name of Father and Mother Divine, I receive the attunement to the Fifth Seal of the Sun'. 'The Creator improves my creativity'.

Names of God for Attunement: Hei.Reish.Yod (ה.ר.י), Yod.Reish.Tav (י.ר.ת), Lamed.Alef.Vav (ל.א.ו), Hei.Zain.Yod (ה.ז.י)

Activation (After First Time): 'In the Names of Father and Mother Divine, and of the Great King Solomon, I activate the Fifth Seal of the Sun'.

6th. Seal of The Sun: *Power of invisibility. Will help you become invisible and disappear from the people around you. Also helps to amend your personal integrity.*

'Make their eyes dark so that they do not see; and let their loins tremble continually' (Psalm 69:24). 'They have eyes, but they do not see' (Psalm 135:16).

Feel connection with the Seal, then say:

'May I disappear to the sight of man and beast. Amen'

Attunement (First Time): 'In the Name of Father and Mother Divine, I receive the attunement to the Sixth Sea of the Sun. The Creator helps me to become invisible to those I wish not to see me.

Names of God for Attunement: Yod.Zayin.Lamed (י.ז. ל), Peh.Vav.Yod (פ.ו.י), Hei.Reish.Yod (ה.ר.י), Lamed.Vav.Vav (ל.ו.ו)

Activation (After First Time): 'In the Names of Father and Mother Divine, and of the Great King Solomon, I activate the Sixth Seal of the Sun'.

7th. Seal of The Sun: *Release from addictions. Releases internal and external influences that bind you, blockages, binding to people, dependency on negative desires or addictions and opens the way to success.*

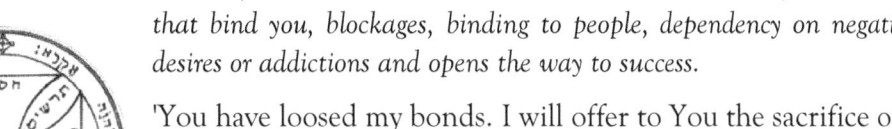

'You have loosed my bonds. I will offer to You the sacrifice of thanksgiving. And will call upon the Name of the Lord' (Psalm 116: 16, 17).

Feel connection with the Seal, then say:

'I invoke the Seraphim, the Cherubim, and the Angels Ariel, Tharsis, Chasan, Arel, Phorlakh and Taliahad. Go you of the great angelic orders, go and do my bidding and unbind me in the name of the great King Solomon. Amen'.

Attunement (First Time): 'In the Name of Father and Mother Divine, I receive the attunement to the Seventh Seal of the Sun. Thanks to the Creator, I am free from any prison'.

Names of God for Attunement: Vav.Hei.Vav (ו.ה.ו), Peh.Hei.Lamed (פ.ה. ל), Lamed.Hei.Cheit (ל.ה.ח), Alef.Nun.Yod (א.נ.י)

Activation (After First Time): 'In the Names of Father and Mother Divine, and of the Great King Solomon, I activate the Seventh Seal of the Sun'.

The Seals of The Moon

Controls the Weather, Brings Rain, Offers Protection from Natural Disasters, Grants Mystical Knowledge.

Day of Week: Monday. Perform ritual on a Monday.
Candle Colour: Silver
Metal It Presides Over: Silver
Number of Seals: 6
The Altar of The Moon: Place the Seal in the middle.
                        Place a silver candle on the right side.
                        Place the incense on the left side. Always face East.

Primary Spirits/Angels Together with Areas of Influence:

1- Schioel -   Helps with lawsuits and grants various legal protections.
2- Vaol -   Helps cultivate creative talents. Bestows success in general.
3- Yashiel -   Helps with business endeavours.
4- Vehiel -   Helps with astral projection.
5- Abariel -   Helps invoking other spirits. Protects against natural disasters.
6- Aub -   Protects us from evil entities during our sleep and always. Spiritual knowledge.
7- Vevaphel -   Protects us from evil entities during our sleep and at all times. Spiritual knowledge.
8- Yahel -   Grants mystical wisdom and knowledge. Also, mystical and magical powers.
9- Sophiel -   Grants knowledge of herbs, stones and animal spirits, and all things in nature.
10- Iachadiel - Banishes unwanted spiritual visitors. Helps summoning the dead.
11- Azarel -   Grants power to contact the spirit world to get answers in our dreams.

These Six Pentacles/Seals give you:

Seal 1: Opens Doors to Success, Cancels Spells.
Seal 2: Protection from Natural Disasters.
Seal 3: Protection from Poltergeists and Hauntings.
Seal 4: Defends from Evil and Teaches About Crystals and Herbs.
Seal 5: Protection During Sleep and Answers in Dreams.
Seal 6: Brings Rain, Controls the Weather.

The Seals of the Moon Chart

1st. Seal of the Moon: *Opens doors to success, cancels spells, opens all doors and locks, releases any blockages, barriers, evil eye or spells and bring you to a new path of success.*

'He has broken the gates of brass and smitten the bars of iron in sunder' (Psalm 107:16).

'I invoke the angels: Schioel, Vaol, Yashiel and Vehiel'.

Feel connection with the Seal, then say:

'Go you angels of this mighty seal, go and fulfill my request and guide me in the name of the great King Solomon. Amen'.

Attunement (First Time): 'In the Name of Father and Mother Divine, I receive the attunement to the 1st. Seal of the Moon'. 'Now my vision is clear, and the doors are open'.

Names of God for Attunement: Cheit.Ayin.Mem (ח.ע.ם), Peh.Vav.Yod (פ.ו.י), Samech.Yod.Teit – (ס.י.ט), Lamed.Caf.Beit (ל.כ.ב)

Activation (After First Time): 'In the Names of Father and Mother Divine, and of the Great King Solomon, I activate the 1st. Seal of the Moon'.

2nd. Seal of the Moon: *Protection from natural disasters. Protection from natural disasters, sea storms, earthquakes and lightning, storms at travel and sailing.*

'In Elohim have I put my trust, I will not fear, what can man do unto me? (Psalm 56:11-13).

'Oh protector angel Abariel I ask you in the name of the great King Solomon, you protect us from all of nature's whims. Be my protector'.

Feel connection with the Seal, then say:

'By this great seal shall it be so'.

Attunement (First Time): 'In the Name of Father and Mother Divine, I receive the attunement to the 2nd. Seal of the Moon'.

'I invoke the Creator's power to protect me from any calamity'.

Names of God for Attunement: Yod.Zayin.Lamed (י.ז. ל), Yod.Lamed.Yod (י.ל.י), Lamed.Alef.Vav (ל.א.ו), Alef.Yod.Ayin (א.י.ע)

Activation (After First Time): 'In the Names of Father and Mother Divine, and of the Great King Solomon, I activate the 2nd. Seal of the Moon'.

3rd. Seal of the Moon: *Protection from poltergeists and hauntings. Protection from natural disasters, sea storms, earthquakes and lightning, storms at travel and sailing.*

'Be pleased O God to deliver me, O God make haste to help me' (Psalm 40:13).

'I invoke the angels Aub and Vevaphel to protect me from all spirits that wish to harm me, or my loved ones. By this great seal shall it be so'.

Feel connection with the Seal, then say:

'Oh great angels go forth in front of me and protect me and my loved ones, from the evils that have come from the other side. Amen'.

Attunement (First Time): 'In the Name of Father and Mother Divine, I receive the attunement to the 3rd. Seal of the Moon. I invoke the power of the Creator to protect me from any danger'.

Names of God for Attunement: Yod.Zayin.Lamed (י.ז. ל), Yod.Lamed.Yod (י.ל.י), Nun.Lamed.Caf (נ.ל.ך), Yod.Lamed.Hei (י. ל.ה)

Activation (After First Time): 'In the Names of Father and Mother Divine, and of the Great King Solomon, I activate the 3rd. Seal of the Moon'.

4th. Seal of the Moon: *Defends from evil and teaches about crystals and herbs. Guards the body and mind from any harm and injury.*

'Let them be confounded who persecute me and let me not be confounded; let them fear and not I' (Psalm 35:4)
'Oh great God Eheieh Asher Eheieh, that is the Name you said unto Moses, your faithful servant. Teach unto me the secrets of the powers of nature. May the stones and plants whisper their secrets in my soul'.

Feel connection with the Seal, then say:

'I now invoke the angels Yahel and Sofiel to teach me the wonderful works of nature and the properties therein. By this great seal shall it be so'.

Attunement (First Time): 'In the Name of Father and Mother Divine, I receive the attunement to the 4th Seal of the Moon. I invoke the power of the Creator to protect me from any injury and to give me the wisdom of nature'.

Names of God for Attunement: Caf.Hei.Tav (כ.ה.ת), Lamed.Alef.Vav (ל.א.ו), Yod.Yod.Yod (י.י.י), Vav.Mem.Beit (ו.מ.ב)

Activation (After First Time): 'In the Names of Father and Mother Divine, and of the Great King Solomon, I activate the 4th. Seal of the Moon'.

5th. Seal of the Moon: *Protection during sleep and answers in dreams. Strengthens the spirit as it ascends to higher realms during sleep, guards from evil spirits and nightmares, provides deep sleep and clear insights from dreams.*

'May God rise and His enemies be scattered; that those who hate Him may flee before Him' (Psalm 68:1).
'Oh, great God YHVH-ELOHIM, that is the Name You revealed to Jacob, who had visions in his sleep. I ask that I too will be recipient of great visions in my sleep.
By this seal shall it be so'.

Feel connection with the Seal, then say:

'I now invoke the angels Iachadiel and Azarel to protect me at night from spirits that lie, and to reveal me what I need to know, during my sleep. By this seal of the great King Solomon shall it be so'.

Attunement (First Time): 'In the Name of Father and Mother Divine, I receive the attunement to the 5th. Seal of the Moon'. 'I invoke the power of the Creator to protect my sleep and to give me understanding of my dreams'.

Names of God for Attunement: Lamed.Lamed.Hei (ל.ל. ה), Hei.Reish.Yod (ה.ר.י), Hei.Zain.Yod (ה.ז.י), Mem.Yod.Caf (מ.י.כ)

Activation (After First Time): 'In the Names of Father and Mother Divine, and of the Great King Solomon, I activate the 5th. Seal of the Moon'.

6th. Seal of the Moon: *Brings rain, controls the weather. Carries the gracefulness of water, showering blessed rains, and guards against drought, hunger and poverty.*

'All the fountains of the great depth were broken...And the rain fell upon the earth' (Genesis 7:11-12).
Feel connection with the Seal, then say:
'By the great power of the Moon, I will control the weather as did the Great and Mighty King Solomon'.

Attunement (First Time): 'In the Name of Father and Mother Divine, I receive the attunement to the 6th. Seal of the Moon'. 'I invoke the power of the Creator to remove famine and rain abundance within me'.

Names of God for Attunement: Samech.Alef.Lamed (ס.א.ל), Hei.Kof.Mem (ה.ק.ם), Reish.Hei.Ayin (ר.ה.ע), Nun.Nun.Alef (נ.נ.א)

Activation (After First Time): 'In the Names of Father and Mother Divine, and of the Great King Solomon, I activate the 6th. Seal of the Moon'.

The Seals of Mars

These Seals give you magical and spiritual powers and helps you control evil forces. They have the property of making invulnerable those who wear them with reverence. They give extraordinary strength and vigour.

Day of Week: Tuesday. Perform ritual on a Tuesday.
Candle Colour: Red
Metal It Presides Over: Iron
Number of Seals: 7
The Altar of Mars: Place the Seal in the middle.
                     Place a red candle on the right side.
                     Place the incense on the left side. Always face East.

Primary Spirits/Angels Together with Areas of Influence:

1- Madimiel- Vanquishes poverty, hunger, and fear.
2- Bartzachiah- Helps attain your ambitions without overdoing it.
3- Eschiel - Helps us fight addiction. Prevents us from becoming addicted to power.
4- Ithuriel- Helps us fight addiction. Prevents us from becoming addicted to power.

These Seven Pentacles/Seals give you:

Seal 1: Passion to Succeed in Chosen Path.
Seal 2: Heals Diseases, Pain and Injuries.
Seal 3: Success in Negotiations.
Seal 4: Victory in Competitions.
Seal 5: Magic Powers and Protection.
Seal 6: Turns Opponents' Weapons Against Them.
Seal 7: Confuses and Binds Adversaries.

The Second Seal of Mars

Heals Diseases, Pain and Injuries. Heals all kinds of diseases, pain and injuries. The seal should be applied unto he afflicted area of the body.

Instructions

- ☐ Perform ritual on a Tuesday, a few minutes before sunrise.
- ☐ Set up an Altar on the East as such: Place the Seal in the middle.
- ☐ Place red candle on the right side.
- ☐ Place the incense on the left side.
- ☐ Light the candle.
- ☐ Light the incense.
- ☐ Pick up the seal and hold it.
- ☐ Think, imagine and feel what it is you want.
- ☐ Then, proceed with the following prayers.

Attunement

The Attunement is Performed once, that is, the First Time you work with the seal

'In the Name of Father and Mother Divine, I receive the attunement to the Second Seal of Mars'.

'I invoke the power of the Creator to heal my body, mind, and spirit. Healing energy fills all of my organs, body and soul. I am functioning perfectly'.

Names of God for Attunement

5. Mem.Hei.Shin   4. Ayin.Lamed.Mem   61. Vav.Mem.Beit   2. Yod.Lamed.Yod

Leave the Talisman on the Altar until the candle and incense are extinguished. Then, you are free to wear the Talisman, or use it as you please, such as put it in your pocket, or leave it on the Altar, whatever is most appropriate for you

Activation

The Activation is performed every time you work with the seal

'In the Names of The Father and Mother Divine, and of the Great King Solomon, I activate the 2nd. Seal of Mars'.

'In Him was life, and the life was the light of man' (John 1:4).

Sit in silence and feel the power of God coursing through you. Visualize the power coming through the top of your head and out of your hands into the seal. Watch it glow. Place the Talisman down and say:

'In gratitude I come before You, Yahweh-Elohim of the universe, I know that you will grant this request for me through this holy Talisman of the great King Solomon. Amen'

The Seals of Mars Chart

1st. Seal of Mars: *Passion to succeed in chosen path. Will enhance courage, enthusiasm, ambition and passion for your occupation to succeed in your chosen path.*

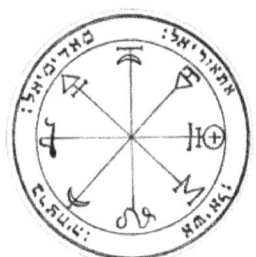

'I invoke the angels: Madimiel, Bartzachiah, Eschiel, and Ithuriel'.

Feel connection with the Seal, then say:

'Go you angels of this mighty seal, go and fulfill my request and guide me in the name of the great King Solomon. Amen'.

Attunement (First Time): 'In the Name of Father and Mother Divine, I receive the attunement to the 1st. Seal of Mars'.

'I am grateful to the Creator for the courage He gives me. All the inhibitions, fears, and restraints that have held me back are dissolving'.

Names of God for Attunement: Reish.Hei.Ayin (ר.ה.ע), Vav.Vav.Lamed (ו.ו.ל), Lamed.Caf.Beit (ל.כ.ב), Mem.Beit.He (מ.ב.ה)

Activation (After First Time): 'In the Names of Father and Mother Divine, and of the Great King Solomon, I activate the 1st. Seal of Mars'.

2nd. Seal of Mars: *Heals diseases, pain and injuries. Heals all kinds of diseases, pain and injuries. The seal should be applied unto the afflicted area of the body.*

'In Him was life, and the life was the light of man' (John 1:4). Feel connection with the Seal, then say:

'In gratitude I come before You, Yahweh-Elohim of the universe, I know that you will grant this wish for me through this holy Talisman of the great King Solomon'.

Attunement (First Time): 'In the Name of Father and Mother Divine, I receive the attunement to the 2nd. Seal of Mars'.

'I invoke the power of the Creator to heal my body, mind, and spirit. Healing energy fills all of my organs, body and soul that are fully functioning'.

Names of God for Attunement: Mem.Hei.Shin (מ.ה.ש), Ayin.Lamed.Mem (ע.ל.ם), Vav.Mem.Beit (ו.מ.ב), Yod.Lamed.Yod (י.ל.י)

Activation (After First Time): 'In the Names of Father and Mother Divine, and of the Great King Solomon, I activate the 2nd. Seal of Mars'.

3rd. Seal of Mars: *Success in negotiations. Helps you overcome your opponents and subdue resistance, bring success in negotiations and conflict resolution.*

'Who is so great a God as our God? (Psalm 77:13).

Feel connection with the Seal, then say:

'In gratitude I come before You, El-Shaddai-Eloha of the Universe. I know that You will grant this wish for me through this holy Talisman of the great King Solomon'.

Attunement (First Time): 'In the Name of Father and Mother Divine, I receive the attunement to the 3rd. Seal of Mars'.

'Negative people and situations that oppose me vanish and have no influence on me. I am guarded and protected by the Creator of all'.

Names of God for Attunement: Caf.Hei.Tav (כ.ה.ת), Lamed.Alef.Vav (ל.א.ו), Lamed.Vav.Vav (ל.ו.ו), Lamed.Caf.Beit (ל.כ.ב)

Activation (After First Time): 'In the Names of Father and Mother Divine, and of the Great King Solomon, I activate the 3rd. Seal of Mars'.

4th. Seal of Mars: *Victory in competitions. Victory in a any argument or competition, gives courage and power in trials and quarrels, and supports good decision-making.*

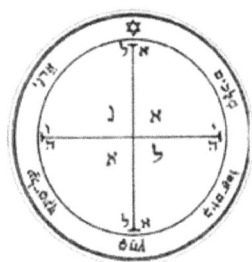

'The Lord at your right hand shall wound even Kings in the day of His wrath' (Psalm 110:5).

Feel connection with the Seal, then say:

'In gratitude I come before you Agla-Adonai-El, of the Universe. I know that you will grant this wish for me through this holy Talisman of the great King Solomon'.

Attunement (First Time): 'In the Name of Father and Mother Divine, I receive the attunement to the 4th. Seal of Mars'.

'I transcend my weaknesses, while my inner strength increases. I am filled with love and self-confidence'.

Names of God for Attunement: Mem.Nun.Dalet (מ.נ.ד), Lamed.Caf.Beit (ל.כ.ב), Dalet.Nun.Yod (ד.נ.י), Mem.Yod.Caf (מ.י.כ)

Activation (After First Time): 'In the Names of Father and Mother Divine, and of the Great King Solomon, I activate the 4th. Seal of Mars'.

5th. Seal of Mars: *Magic Powers and protection. Gives you magical and spiritual powers and helps you control evil and dark forces.*

'You shall go upon the lion and adder, the young lion and the dragon shall you tread under your feet' (Psalm 91:13).

Feel connection with the Seal, then say:

'In gratitude I come before You, King of the Universe,
I know that You will grant this wish for me through this Holy Talisman of the great King Solomon'.

Attunement (First Time): 'In the Name of Father and Mother Divine, I receive the attunement to the 5th. Seal of Mars'.

'My negative thoughts are cleansed, despair, frustration, and sadness leave.
I am protected from the harmful forces that try to harm me, and from all dangers and decrees. The Creator protects me through his angels'.

Names of God for Attunement: Yod.Lamed.Yod (י.ל.י), Lamed.Alef.Vav (ל.א.ו), Lamed.Vav.Vav (ל.ו.ו), Yod.Yod.Yod (י.י.י)

Activation (After First Time): 'In the Names of Father and Mother Divine, and of the Great King Solomon, I activate the 5th. Seal of Mars'.

6th. Seal of Mars: *Turns opponents' weapons against them. Protects against harm and threat and causes your opponent's own weapons to turn against him.*

'His sword shall enter into his own heart, and his bows shall be broken' (Psalm 37:15).

Feel connection with the Seal, then say:

'In gratitude I come before You, Yahweh the great protector of the universe. I know that You will grant this wish for me through this holy Talisman of the great King Solomon'.

Attunement (First Time): 'In the Name of Father and Mother Divine, I receive the attunement to the 6th. Seal of Mars'.

'Enemies, adversaries and negative presences disappear from my life. Nothing hinders or prevents me from achieving my goals'.

Names of God for Attunement: Yod.Lamed.Yod (י.ל.י), Lamed.Caf.Beit (ל.כ.ב), Cheit.Ayin.Mem (ח.ע.ם), Hei.Yod.Yod (ה.י.י)

Activation (After First Time): 'In the Names of Father and Mother Divine, and of the Great King Solomon, I activate the 6th. Seal of Mars'.

7th. Seal of Mars: *Confuses and blinds your adversaries. Gives you the ability to confuse your adversaries and blind their vision so they can not harm you.*

'He gave them hail for rain and flaming fire in their land. He smote their vines also, and their fig-trees' (Psalm 105:32).

Feel connection with the Seal, then say:

'In gratitude I come before You El-Yee-Ya, the great controller of the tempests. I know that You will grant this request for me through this holy Talisman of the great King Solomon'.

Attunement (First Time): 'In the Name of Father and Mother Divine, I receive the attunement to the 7th. Seal of Mars'.

The light of the Creator protects me from anyone who wants to hurt me. The forces of evil cannot approach me, any curse or occult attack vanishes in the light of the Creator.

Names of God for Attunement: Alef.Yod.Ayin (א.י.ע), Reish.Alef.Hei (ר.א.ה), Cheit.Ayin.Mem (ח.ע.ם), Lamed.Alef.Vav (ל.א.ו)

Activation (After First Time): 'In the Names of Father and Mother Divine, and of the Great King Solomon, I activate the 7th. Seal of Mars'.

The Seals of Mercury

These Seals help you to attain the impossible.
They help you to have harmony and unity with your loved ones.
They help increase your personal magnetism.
They make you eloquent They give you knowledge of science and good memory.
They reveal you answers through dreams (when placing them under your pillow).

Day of Week: Mercury. Perform ritual on a Wednesday.
Candle Colour: Orange
Metal It Presides Over: Quicksilver
Number of Seals: 5
The Altar of Mercury: Place the Seal in the middle.
                         Place an orange candle on the right side.
                         Place the incense on the left side. Always face East.

Primary Spirits/Angels Together with Areas of Influence:

1- Yekahel-   Helps to increase your personal magnetism.
2- Agiel-   Helps to increase your personal magnetism.
3- Boel -   Commands the four corners of the Earth. Helps attain the impossible.
4- Kokaviel-   Grants knowledge of science, magic, and alchemy.
5- Gheoriah-   Helps you to learn the deep mysteries of the spirit.
6- Savaniah-   Helps you to learn the deep mysteries of the spirit.
7- Hokmahiel- His name means the wisdom of God. Helps with literary skills.

These Six Pentacles/Seals give you:

Seal 1: Personal Magnetism.
Seal 2: Attain the Impossible.
Seal 3: Influence with Words.
Seal 4: Wisdom and Knowledge.
Seal 5: Opens Doors and Portals (Spiritual and Physical).

The Seals of Mercury Chart

1st. Seal of Mercury: *Personal magnetism. Gives personal charm and charisma and magnetize people to you. Good for attracting a soul mate or for any social purpose.*

'I invoke the angels Yekahel and Agiel. Make me irresistible to the people I encounter, and make me mentally strong, so I may appreciate my power. Amen'.

Feel connection with the Seal, then say:

'In gratitude I thank you, Oh mighty angels. I know that you will grant this wish for me through this holy Talisman of the great King Solomon'.

Attunement (First Time): 'In the Name of Father and Mother Divine, I receive the attunement to the 1st. Seal of Mercury'.

'I am grateful to the Creator for the charm he gives me. I now express my divine beauty'.

Names of God for Attunement: Caf.Vav.Kof (כ.ו.ק), Shin.Alef.Hei (ש.א.ה), Reish.Hei.Ayin (ר.ה.ע), Mem.Yod.Hei (מ.י.ה)

Activation (After First Time): 'In the Names of Father and Mother Divine, and of the Great King Solomon, I activate the 1st. Seal of Mercury'.

2nd. Seal of Mercury: *Attain the impossible. Helps you attain the impossible and fulfill your wishes even when they are contrary to the laws of nature.*

'I invoke the angel Boel, who commands the four corners of the Earth. By the power of this great seal of the great King Solomon, I implore you to help me remedy this pressing issue. Amen'.

Feel connection with the Seal, then say:

'In gratitude I thank you Boel. I know that you will grant this wish for me through this holy Talisman of the great King Solomon'.

Attunement (First Time): 'In the Name of Father and Mother Divine, I receive the attunement to the 2nd. Seal of Mercury'.

'I invoke the Creator's power to make me fertile so that I can accomplish what I desire'.

Names of God for Attunment: Samech.Yod.Teit – (ס.י.ט), Vav.Hei.Vav (ו.ה.ו), Nun.Tav.Hei (נ.ת.ה), Vav.Shin.Reish (ו.ש.ר)

Activation (After First Time): 'In the Names of Father and Mother Divine, and of the Great King Solomon, I activate the 2nd. Seal of Mercury'.

3rd. Seal of Mercury: *Influence with words. Enhances the eloquence and expressional skills and helps you influence people with your written or verbal words.*

'I invoke the angels: Kokaviel, Gheoriah, Savaniah and Hokmahiel to give me the power to learn and write with ease and great creativity, so that I can gain the love and admiration of others through my work. Amen'.

Feel connection with the Seal, then say:

'Go you angels of this mighty seal, go and fulfill my request and guide me in the name of the great King Solomon. Amen'.

Attunement (First Time): 'In the Name of Father and Mother Divine, I receive the attunement to the 3rd. Seal of Mercury'.

'By the Creator's will I now express all my creativity'

Names of God for Attunement: Hei.Zain.Yod (ה.ז.י), Ayin.Lamed.Mem (ע.ל.מ), Mem.Lamed.Hei (מ.ל.ה), Yod.Yod.Zayin (י.י.ז)

Activation (After First Time): 'In the Names of Father and Mother Divine, and of the Great King Solomon, I activate the 3rd. Seal of Mercury'.

4th. Seal of Mercury: *Wisdom and knowledge. Will help you acquire wisdom, know and understand the thoughts of others and narrow the gaps between you and your loved ones.*

'Wisdom and virtue are in his house, and the knowledge of all things remains with him forever' (Psalm 112:3).

'God, fix Thou the volatile, and let there be unto the void restriction'.

'I invoke the Name of God: EL, the Mighty God of creation. He who has brought forth knowledge of all kinds. Bless me by the merits of this great seal of the great King Solomon with the knowledge and wisdom I require'

Feel connection with the Seal, then say:

'Thank You El, for You Are the granter of all knowledge'.

Attunement (First Time): 'In the Name of Father and Mother Divine, I receive the attunement to the 4th. Seal of Mercury'.

'Divine wisdom now shines through me'.

Names of God for Attunement: Hei.Reish.Yod (ה.ר.י), Nun.Tav.Hei (נ.ת.ה), Reish.Yod.Yod (ר.י.י), Mem.Cheit.Yod (מ.ח.י)

Activation (After First Time): 'In the Names of Father and Mother Divine, and of the Great King Solomon, I activate the 4th. Seal of Mercury'.

5th. Seal of Mercury: *Opens doors and portals (spiritual and physical). Breaks all blockages and barriers, overcomes resistance, or defeatism and opens the door to success.*

'Lift up your heads, you gate; lift them up, you ancient doors, that the King of glory may come in' (Psalm 24:9).

'I invoke the Name of God: YHVH-EL, the mighty God of Creation, and Father of us all, He who has no barrier.

Bless me by the merits of this great seal of Your servant King Solomon with the ability to open and enter spiritual portals that have been closed to those who are uninitiated. Amen'.

Feel connection with the Seal, then say:

'Thank You YHVH-EL our Father, for You Are the Guardian of all knowledge and dimensions'.

Attunement (First Time): 'In the Name of Father and Mother Divine, I receive the attunement to the 5th. Seal of Mercury'.

'All doors are now open to me and obstacles are removed'.

Names of God for Attunement: Samech.Alef.Lamed (ס.א.ל), Lamed.Caf.Beit (ל.כ.ב), Reish.Hei.Ayin (ר.ה.ע), Yod.Reish.Tav (י.ר.ת)

Activation (After First Time): 'In the Names of Father and Mother Divine, and of the Great King Solomon, I activate the 5th. Seal of Mercury'.

The Seals of Jupiter

They bring Success and Financial Abundance, Psychic Powers and Protection.

Day of Week: Thursday. Perform ritual on a Thursday.
Candle Colour: Brass
Metal It Presides Over: Blue (azure)
Number of Seals: 7
The Altar of Jupiter: Place the Seal in the middle.
Place a blue candle on the right side.
Place the incense on the left side. Always face East.

Primary Spirits/Angels Together with Areas of Influence:

1- Netoniel- Helps you achieve fame and notoriety.
2- Devachiah- Bestows balance in all things. Also, inner peace.
3- Tzedeqiah- Brings riches, glory and honour.
4- Parasiel- He is the lord over vast treasures.
5- Adoniel- He increases luck in all things financial.
6- Bariel- He is the giver of long life and health.
7- Serph- Which is from the order of angels, which means fiery ones.
8- Kerub- Which is from the order of the cherubim angels.
9- Ariel - The lion of God and protector angel, and angel of new beginnings.
10- Tharsis- Helps with life choices and decision making. Helps to avoid danger.

These six pentacles/seals give you:

Seal 1: Success and Financial Abundance.
Seal 2: Glory and Peace of Mind.
Seal 3: Clears and Protects Houses.
Seal 4: Great Financial Abundance.
Seal 5: Spiritual and Psychic Powers.
Seal 6: Protection from Earthy Dangers.
Seal 7: Power Over Those Who Attempt to Fail You.

The Seals of Jupiter Chart

1st. Seal of Jupiter: *Success and financial abundance. Places you on a new path of success, attracts abundance and good livelihood, richness and material gain.*

'I invoke the Angels: Netoniel (fame), Devachiah (equilibrium and peace), Tzedeqiah (riches, glory and honour), and Parasiel (great treasures).

Feel connection with the Seal, then say:

'Go you angels of this mighty seal, go and bring forth abundance in the name of the great King Solomon. Amen'.

Attunement (First Time): 'In the Name of Father and Mother Divine, I receive the attunement to the 1st. Seal of Jupiter'.

'My life enters a path of manifestation of abundance, and I am ready to receive it. I let go of everything I don't need any more to make room for abundance'.

Names of God for Attunement: Samech.Alef.Lamed (ס.א.ל), Caf.Hei.Tav (כ.ה.ת), Vav.Vav.Lamed (ו.ו.ל), Reish.Hei.Ayin (ר.ה.ע)

Activation (After First Time): 'In the Names of Father and Mother Divine, and of the Great King Solomon, I activate the 1st.Seal of Jupiter'.

2nd. Seal of Jupiter: *Glory and peace of mind. Helps to acquire glory, dignity and tranquillity, induces balance of body and mind.*

'Well-being and riches are in his house, and his righteousness endures forever' (Psalm 112:3).

Feel connection with the Seal, then say:

'In gratitude I come before You Yahweh-Ehieh, with Your power I attract wealth and success to me. You are my Father, the great Lord and Father of all there is. I know You will bring me the prosperity that I request through this holy Talisman of the Great King Solomon.'

Attunement (First Time): 'In the Name of Father and Mother Divine, I receive the attunement to the 2nd. Seal of Jupiter'.

I am worthy of receiving abundance from the universe effortlessly and the divine loving light rebalances me and purifies me.

Names of God for Attunement: Mem.Hei.Shin (מ.ה.ש), Caf.Hei.Tav (כ.ה.ת), Alef.Lamed.Dalet (א.ל.ד), Lamed.Alef.Vav (ל.א.ו)

Activation (After First Time): 'In the Names of Father and Mother Divine, and of the Great King Solomon, I activate the 2nd. Seal of Jupiter'.

3rd. Seal of Jupiter: *Clears and protects houses. Defends and protects against opponents and evil spirits, curses and spells in the house and around it.*

'They that trust in the LORD shall be as Mount Zion, which cannot be removed, but abides forever' (Psalm 125:1)

Feel connection with the Seal, then say:

'In gratitude I come before You, Yahweh-Adonai, the great protector and implore You to protect me from the spirits and entities that wish to harm me, by the power vested in this seal, You will protect me. Amen'.

Attunement (First Time): 'In the Name of Father and Mother Divine, I receive the attunement to the 3rd. Seal of Jupiter'.

The Creator protects me from all harmful forces and evil spirits. All negative forces disappear from my life.

Names of God for Attunement: Yod.Yod.Yod (י.י.י), Caf.He.Tav (כ.ה.ת), Alef.Lamed.Dalet (א.ל.ד), Lamed.Alef.Vav (ל.א.ו)

Activation (After First Time): 'In the Names of Father and Mother Divine, and of the Great King Solomon, I activate the 3rd. Seal of Jupiter'.

4th. Seal of Jupiter: *Great financial abundance. Helps to enjoy the best treasures of life, comfort and honour, enrichment with abundance and good harvest.*

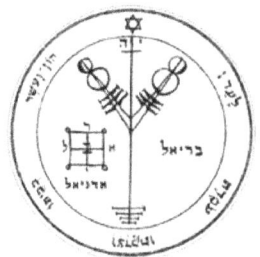

'Wealth and riches are in His house, and His righteousness endures forever' (Psalm 112:3).

'I invoke the angels: Adoniel (who increases luck in all financial matters) and Bariel (the giver of long life and health).

Feel connection with the Seal, then say:

'In gratitude I come before angels Adoniel and Bariel for listening to my request, in the name of the great King Solomon and God Almighty you will grant this request for me'.

Attunement (First Time): 'In the Name of Father and Mother Divine, I receive the attunement to the 4th. Seal of Jupiter'.

'I am blessed by the abundance of the Creator; his light floods me.
I let go of doubts, fears, and concerns about my sustenance in front of the Creator who dissolves them'.

Names of God for Attunement: Samech.Alef.Lamed (ס.א.ל), Yod.Reish.Tav (י.ר.ת), Vav.Hei.Vav (ו.ה.ו), Alef.Lamed.Dalet (א.ל.ד)

Activation (After First Time): 'In the Names of Father and Mother Divine, and of the Great King Solomon, I activate the 4th. Seal of Jupiter'.

5th. Seal of Jupiter: *Spiritual and psychic powers. To remove the veils from knowledge, revel Divine secrets, gain spiritual and psychic powers and fulfill your visions and dreams.*

'While I was among the exiles by the Kebar River, the heavens were opened, and I saw visions of God' (Ezekiel 1:1).

Feel connection with the Seal.

Attunement (First Time): 'In the Name of Father and Mother Divine, I receive the attunement to the 5th. Seal of Jupiter'.

'I climb the stair of my spiritual evolution, my eyes open, angels and sacred entities are revealed to me and guide me. I see beyond all illusions'.

Names of God for Attunement: Hei.Reish.Yod (ה.ר.י), Shin.Alef.Hei (ש.א.ה), Reish.Alef.Hei (ר.א.ה), Hei.Zain.Yod (ה.ז.י)

Activation (After First Time): 'In the Names of Father and Mother Divine, and of the Great King Solomon, I activate the 5th. Seal of Jupiter'.

6th. Seal of Jupiter: *Protection from earthly dangers. Provides protection against all earthly dangers, accidents and injury, keeps perils away wherever you go.*

'They have pierced my hands and my feet. I can count all my bones' (Psalm 22:16-17).

'I invoke the Seraphim, the Cherubim, the angels Ariel and Tharsis, to protect me in all my ways, in the name of the great King Solomon'.

Feel connection with the Seal.

'Go you of the great angelic orders, go and do my bidding, protect me from all harm in the name of the great King Solomon. Amen'.

Attunement (First Time): 'In the Name of Father and Mother Divine, I receive the attunement to the 6th. Seal of Jupiter'.

'Any harmful power, every person, word, or negative act cannot hurt me.
I release all the fears and anxieties of my life, I am full of courage and values'.

Names of God for Attunement: Yod.Lamed.Hei (י.ל.ה), Yod.Yod.Yod (י.י.י), Mem.Nun.Dalet (מ.נ.ד), Lamed.Caf.Beit (ל.כ.ב)

Activation (After First Time): 'In the Names of Father and Mother Divine, and of the Great King Solomon, I activate the 6th. Seal of Jupiter'.

7th. Seal of Jupiter: *Power over those who attempt to fail you. Has great power against poverty, famine, loss of property and people who attempt to fail you.*

'Raise the poor from the mire and bring the needy from the dunghill, to sit with the princes of his people' (Psalm 113:7).

Feel connection with the Seal, then say:

'In gratitude I come before You, Lord of the Universe.
I know that You will grant this request for me through this holy Talisman of the great King Solomon. Amen'.

Attunement (First Time): 'In the Name of Father and Mother Divine, I receive the attunement to the 7th. Seal of Jupiter'.

'I ask the Creator to rectify my soul and purify it from impurities, harmful forces, and my fears. I am free from all difficulties and anxieties, I am protected and enveloped by divine protective light'.

Names of God for Attunement: Lamed.Alef.Vav (ל.א.ו), Cheit.Hei.Vav (ח.ה.ו), Nun.Lamed.Caf (נ.ל.ך), Alef.Nun.Yod (א.נ.י)

Activation (After First Time): 'In the Names of Father and Mother Divine, and of the Great King Solomon, I activate the 7th. Seal of Jupiter'.

The Seals of Venus

Bring Love and Romance into your life. Enhance your personal magnetism.
Help with Fertility and with Being Fruitful at Work.

Day of Week: Friday. Perform ritual on a Friday.
Candle Colour: Pink, Green
Metal It Presides Over: Copper
Number of Seals: 5
The Altar of Venus: Place the Seal in the middle.
Place a pink candle on the right side.
Place the incense on the left side. Always face East.

Primary Spirits/Angels Together with Areas of Influence:

1- Nogahiel- Helps getting people to fall in love with you.
2- Acheliah- Enhances your personal magnetism.
3- Socodiah - Gives courage in matters of love and interpersonal relationships.
4- Nangariel - Helps you to be in control of your emotions. Brings love and admiration of others.
5- Ruach- Which means Holy Spirit.
6- Achides- Brings love and admiration from others. Helps being fruitful at work.
7- Aegalmiel- Brings love and admiration from others. Helps being fruitful at work.
8- Monachiel - This is an angel of love and romance.
9- Degaliel- Brings love and admiration from others. Helps beings fruitful at work.

These Six Pentacles/Seals give you:

Seal 1: Summons the Right Soul Mate.
Seal 2: Love Among People and with God.
Seal 3: Fertility, Fruitfulness at Work.
Seal 4: Brings People Together.
Seal 5: Love, Attraction and Desire.

The Seals of Venus Chart

1st. Seal of Venus:

Summons the right soulmate. Induces pure love and friendship between people, especially between couples, improves sexual vigour and summons the right soul mate to your life.

'I invoke the angels: Nogahiel, to give me the ability to make friends, (or) to bring me my soul mate.

Acheliah, to enhance my personal magnetism so as to attract the attention of those I wish.

Socodiah, to give me the courage to be more interactive with my fellow man.

Nangariel, to keep my magical abilities high, so I can gain the love and admiration of others'.

Feel connection with the Seal, then say:

'Go you angels of this mighty seal go and fulfill my request and guide me in the name of the great King Solomon'.

Attunement (First Time): 'In the Name of Father and Mother Divine, I receive the attunement to the 1st.Seal of Venus'.

'Thanks to Creator I am surrounded of love and friends'.

Names of God for Attunement: Ayin.Lamed.Mem (ע.ל.מ), Mem.Hei.Shin (מ.ה.ש), Caf.Vav.Kof (כ.ו.ק), Samech.Yod.Teit (ס.י.ט)

Activation (After First Time): 'In the Names of Father and Mother Divine, and of the Great King Solomon, I activate the 1st.Seal of Venus'.

2nd. Seal of Venus:

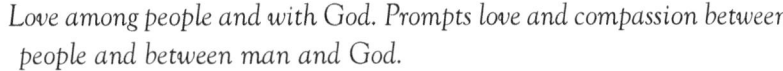

Love among people and with God. Prompts love and compassion between people and between man and God.
Brings its owner dignity, grace and fulfillment of wishes.

'Put me as a sign upon your heart, as a sign of your arm, because love is as strong as death' (Songs of Songs 8:6)

Feel connection with the Seal, then say:

'I have grace and honour. Amen'.

Attunement (First Time): 'In the Name of Father and Mother Divine, I receive the attunement to the 2nd.Seal of Venus'. 'I invoke the Creator's power to achieve the desires of my heart'.

Names of God for Attunement: Alef.Caf.Alef (א.כ.א), Caf.Lamed.Yod (כ.ל.י), Lamed.Hei.Cheit (ל.ה.ח), Mem.Tzadi.Reish (מ.צ.ר)

Activation (After First Time): 'In the Names of Father and Mother Divine, and of the Great King Solomon, I activate the 2nd.Seal of Venus'.

3rd. Seal of Venus: *Fertility, fruitfulness at work. Helps to attract the love of a desirable person, brings love and admiration from those around you, good for all fertility issues, childbirth, fruitfulness at work and career.*

'And the Elohim blessed them, and the Elohim said unto them, 'Be ye fruitful, and multiply, and replenish the Earth and subdue it'. 'Oh Mighty YHVH-Adonai, the most powerful of names, I ask You to give me unlimited personal magnetism, more than I will ever need. Do so by the merit of the Great King Solomon'. 'Oh Mighty angels Ruach, Achides, Aegalmiel, Monachiel, and Dagaliel, I request you by the powers vested in this great seal of King Solomon, to bring me the love and admiration from those around me and make me fruitful at work'.

Feel connection with the Seal, then say:

'In gratitude I come before You YHVH, the Keeper of hearts. I know that You will grant this wish for me through this holy Talisman of the great King Solomon'.

Attunement (First Time): 'In the Name of Father and Mother Divine, I receive the attunement to the 3rd.Seal of Venus'. 'By the Creator's will I now attract my twin soul'.

Names of God for Attunement: Nun.Tav.Hei (נ.ת.ה), Lamed.Caf.Beit (ל.כ.ב), Samech.Alef.Lamed (ס.א.ל), Caf.Vav.Kof (כ.ו.ק)

Activation (After First Time): 'In the Names of Father and Mother Divine, and of the Great King Solomon, I activate the 3rd.Seal of Venus'.

4th. Seal of Venus: *Brings people together. Powerful for bringing people together from remote places and unifying them, helps difficulties in realizing marriage and solves marital problems in good spirits.*

'This is bone of my bones and flesh of my flesh, and they were one flesh' (Genesis 2:23,24). 'Oh Mighty YHVH - You who can soften and harden every person's heart. I ask You to send my loved one my way and have him/her irresistibly attracted to me. Do so by the merit of the Great King Solomon'.

Feel connection with the Seal, then say:

'In gratitude, I come before You, YHVH, the Keeper of hearts. I know that You will grant this wish for me through this holy Talisman of Solomon Your servant'.

Attunement (First Time): 'In the Name of Father and Mother Divine, I receive the attunement to the 4th. Seal of Venus'.

'Divine wisdom now shines through me and I am full of love'.

Names of God for Attunement: Alef.Caf.Alef (א.כ.א), Mem.Beit.Hei (מ.ב.ה), Cheit.Beit.Vav (ח.ב.ו), Mem.Yod.Hei (מ.י.ה)

Activation (After First Time): 'In the Names of Father and Mother Divine, and of the Great King Solomon, I activate the 4th. Seal of Venus'.

5th. Seal of Venus: *Love, attraction and desire. Intensifies the desire of a loved one to you, makes your partner to fulfill your romantic wishes, and helps you become desirable by people.*

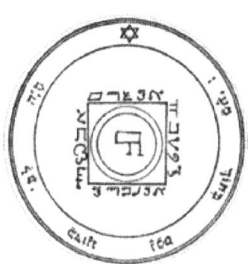

'My heart is like wax; it is melted in the midst of my bowels' (Psalms 22:14).

Feel connection with the Seal, then say:

'My beloved_____ will be attracted to me, by the power of this seal of the great King Solomon'.

Attunement (First Time): 'In the Name of Father and Mother Divine, I receive the attunement to the 5th. Seal of Venus '.

'I am now a pole of attraction for beauty and love'.

Names of God for Attunement: Lamed.Vav.Vav (ל.ו.ו), Mem.Lamed.Hei (מ.ל.ה), Ayin.Mem.Mem (ע.מ.ם), Hei.Reish.Yod (ה.ר.י)

Activation (After First Time): 'In the Names of Father and Mother Divine, and of the Great King Solomon, I activate the 5th. Seal of Venus '.

The Seals of Saturn

Bring Good Luck and Success in Business and Negotiations.
Offers Great Overall Protection.

Day of Week: Saturday. Perform ritual on a Saturday.
Candle Colour: Black, Blue (midnight).
Metal It Presides Over: Lead.
Number of Seals: 7
The Altar of Saturn: Place the Seal in the middle.
Place a black candle on the right side.
Place the incense on the left side. Always face East.

Primary Spirits/Angels Together with Areas of Influence:

1- Omliel- Binds spirits who try to harm you.
2- Anachiel- Protects you from the people who attempt to hurt you. Helps with obtaining confidence.
3- Arauchia- Helps you identify lies and betrayals from others and protects you from those lies.
4- Anatzchia- Helps you from all evils of others.
5- Arehanah- Shows you how to live a proper life.
6- Rakhaniel- Bestows wisdom and will power.
7- Roelhaiphar- Prevents tragedies and bad things.
8- Noaphiel- Protects your house, assets, body and soul.
9- Chayot Ha Kodesh - Holy Living Creatures (order of angels).
10- Auphanim- The Wheels (order of angels).
11- Aralim- The Thrones (order of angels).
12- Chaschmalin - The Brilliant Ones (order of angels).

These Six Pentacles/Seals give you:

Seal 1: Victory on Negotiations.
Seal 2: Success in Business.
Seal 3: Protection from Witchcraft and Psychic Attacks.
Seal 4: Good Decisions in Your Favour.
Seal 5: Protects House, Assets, Body and Soul.
Seal 6: Keeps Enemies Away.
Seal 7: Stops Bad Luck.

The Seals of Saturn Chart

1st. Seal of Saturn: *Victory on negotiations. Defeats opponents at trial and negotiation and forces the rival to be responsive and obedient and fulfill your wishes.*

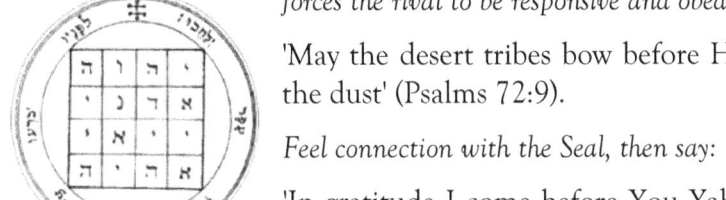

'May the desert tribes bow before Him, and His enemies lick the dust' (Psalms 72:9).

Feel connection with the Seal, then say:

'In gratitude I come before You Yahweh-Adonai. I know that You will grant this wish for me through this holy Talisman of the Great King Solomon.'

Attunement (First Time): 'In the Name of Father and Mother Divine, I receive the attunement to the 1st.Seal of Saturn'.

'I am grateful to the Creator for the persuasive power he gives me'.

Names of God for Attunement: Hei.Zain.Yod (ה.ז.י), Yod.Yod.Zayin (י.י.ז), Mem.Lamed.Hei (מ.ל.ה), Mem.Beit.He (מ.ב.ה)

Activation (After First Time): 'In the Names oif Father and Mother Divine, and of the Great King Solomon, I activate the 1st. Seal of Saturn'.

2nd. Seal of Saturn: *Success in businesses. Gives power in any business engagement, enhances your persuasiveness and finding favour with rivals, helps you succeed in business and debates.*

'His dominion shall be from sea to sea, from the flood to the end of the world' (Psalm 72: 8).

Feel connection with the Seal, then say:

'In the Name of the Almighty God, grant this wish for me through this holy Talisman of Solomon Your servant'.

Attunement (First Time): 'In the Name of Father and Mother Divine, I receive the attunement to the 2nd. Seal of Saturn'.

'I invoke the Creator's power to increase my earnings and to receive subsistence'.
Names of God for Attunement: Samech.Alef.Lamed (ס.א.ל), Samech.Yod.Teit – (ס.י.ט), Mem.Lamed.Hei (מ.ל.ה), Mem.Cheit.Yod (מ.ח.י)

Activation (After First Time): 'In the Names of Father and Mother Divine, and of the Great King Solomon, I activate the 2nd. Seal of Saturn'.

3rd. Seal of Saturn: *Protection from witchcraft and psychic attacks. Protects against detractors who speak ill or you, conspiracies, curses, witchery, evil eye and any trouble imposed by other people.*

'I invoke the angels: Omeliel (who binds the spirits trying to harm me), Anachiel (protects me from people trying to harm me), Arauchia (protects from betrayals), and Anatzachia (protects me from all evils of others).

Feel connection with the Seal, then say:

'Go you angels Omliel, Anachiel, Aruachia and Anatzachia and protect me, and remember this holy seal of the great King Solomon'.

Attunement (First Time): 'In the Name of Father and Mother Divine, I receive the attunement to the 3rd.Seal of Saturn'.

'Evil entities that oppose me vanish and have no influence on me. I am guarded and protected by the Creator's will'.

Names of God for Attunement: Alef.Lamed.Dalet (א.ל.ד), Lamed.Alef.Vav (ל.א.ו), Reish.Yod.Yod (ר.י.י), Cheit.Ayin.Mem (ח.ע.ם)

Activation (After First Time): 'In the Names of Father and Mother Divine, and of the Great King Solomon, I activate the 3rd.Seal of Saturn'.

4th. Seal of Saturn: *Good Decisions in Your Favour. Eliminates detracting forces, brings good news about decisions made in your favour, positive answers for interviews, exams and expectations.*

'Hear, Oh Israel: The LORD our God, the LORD is one (Deut.6:4).

'He wore cursing as his garment; it entered into his body like water, into his bones like oil (Psalms 109:18).

Feel connection with the Seal.

Attunement (First Time): 'In the Name of Father and Mother Divine, I receive the attunement to the 4th. Seal of Saturn'.

'I am filled with love and self-confidence and receive beautiful news'.

Names of God for Attunement: Hei.Reish.Yod (ה.ר.י), Mem.Yod.Hei (מ.י.ה), Samech.Alef.Lamed (ס.א.ל), Vav.Vav.Lamed (ו.ו.ל)

Activation (After First Time): 'In the Names of Father and Mother Divine, and of the Great King Solomon, I activate the 4th. Seal of Saturn'.

5th. Seal of Saturn: *Protects house, assets, body and soul. Guards the house and its contents from burglars, evil forces and damage, protect you precious assets against loss and harm to body and soul.*

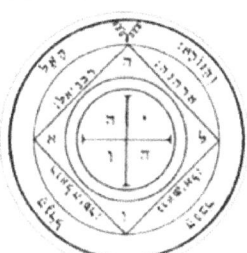

'For the LORD, your God is God of gods and Lord of lords, the great God, and awesome, who shows no partiality and accepts no bribes (Deut.10:17).

'I invoke the angels: Arehanah, Rakhaniel, Roelhaiphar and Noaphiel'.

Feel connection with the Seal, then say:

'Go you angels of this mighty seal, go and protect me from all dangers that may come across my path, in the Name of Eloha-Yahweh. Amen'.

Attunement (First Time): 'In the Name of Father and Mother Divine, I receive the attunement to the 5th.Seal of Saturn'.

'The Creator protects my home and my temple'.

Names of God for Attunement: Lamed.Alef.Vav (ל.א.ו), Alef.Lamed.Dalet (א.ל.ד), Hei.Hei.Ayin (ה.ה.ע), Mem.Nun.Kof (מ.נ.ק)

Activation (After First Time): 'In the Names of Father and Mother Divine, and of the Great King Solomon, I activate the 5th. Seal of Saturn'.

6th. Seal of Saturn: *Keeps enemies away. This seal will inflict fear on a threatening person. Hold it in your right hand and say the enemy's name 7 times.*

'I have delivered him into the hands of the nations, he shall deal with him: I have cast him out according to his wickedness' (Ezekiel 31:11).

Feel connection with the Seal.

Attunement (First Time): 'In the Name of Father and Mother Divine, I receive the attunement to the 6th. Seal of Saturn'.

'Evil forces and negative presences disappear from my life. Nothing stands in my way or prevents me from achieving my goals'.

Names of God for Attunement: Yod.Lamed.Hei (י.ל.ה), Peh.Vav.Yod (פ.ו.י), Yod.Lamed.Yod (י.ל.י), Caf.Hei.Tav (כ.ה.ת)

Activation (After First Time): 'In the Names of Father and Mother Divine, and of the Great King Solomon, I activate the 6th.Seal of Saturn'.

7th. Seal of Saturn: Stops bad luck. This seal will make your words to be heard in heaven. People will listen with respect and awe to what you say and trust your words.

'Then the Earth trembled and shook, the bases of the hills also moved and were shaken, because He was angry' (Psalm 18:7).

'I invoke:
the Chayot Ha Kodesh (the Four Living Creatures),
the Ophanim (the Wheels),
the Erelim (the Mighty Ones, the Thrones),
the Chaschmalin (the Brilliant Ones, the Dominions),
the Seraphim (the Flaming Ones),
the Melachim (the Virtues, the Kings),
the Elohim (the gods, the Principalities),
the Beni Elohim (Sons of the Elohim), and
the Cherubim (the Archangels of Humanity).

Feel connection with the Seal.

Attunement (First Time): 'In the Name of Father and Mother Divine, I receive the attunement to the 7th. Seal of Saturn'.

'Thanks to the Creator I am now heard, in Heaven and on Earth'.

Names of God for Attunement: Mem.Lamed.Hei (מ.ל.ה), Yod.Reish.Tav (י.ר.ת), Nun.Nun. Alef (נ.נ.א), Mem.Beit.Hei (מ.ב.ה)

Activation (After First Time): 'In the Names of Father and Mother Divine, and of the Great King Solomon, I activate the 7th. Seal of Saturn'.

The 72 Names of God and King Solomon's Seals

Sun's Seals

First Seal of the Sun
Yod.Hei.Hei (י.ה. ה)
Mem.Lamed.Hei (מ.ל. ה)
Lamed.Vav.Vav (ל.ו.ו)
Yod.Beit.Mem (י.ב.מ)

Second Seal of the Sun
Cheit.Hei.Vav (ח.ה.ו)
Vav.Vav.Lamed (ו.ו.ל)
Mem.Tzadi.Reish (מ.צ.ר)
Alef.Yod.Ayin (א.י.ע)

Third Seal of the Sun
Samech.Alef.Lamed (ס.א.ל)
Nun.Nun.Alef (נ.נ.א)
Ayin.Nun.Vav (ע.נ.ו)
Yod.Beit.Mem (י.ב.מ)

Fourth Seal of the Sun
Ayin.Shin.Lamed (ע.ש. ל)
Mem.Cheit.Yod (מ.ח.י)
Reish.Alef.Hei (ר.א. ה)
Nun.Tav.Hei (נ.ת. ה)

Fifth Seal of the Sun
Hei.Reish.Yod (ה.ר.י)
Yod.Reish.Tav (י.ר.ת)
Lamed.Alef.Vav (ל.א.ו)
Hei.Zain.Yod (ה.ז.י)

Sixth Seal of the Sun
Yod.Zayin.Lamed (י.ז. ל)
Peh.Vav.Yod (פ.ו.י)
Hei.Reish.Yod (ה.ר.י)
Lamed.Vav.Vav (ל.ו.ו)

Seventh Seal of the Sun
Vav.Hei.Vav (ו.ה.ו)
Peh.Hei.Lamed (פ.ה. ל)
Lamed.Hei.Cheit (ל.ה.ח)
Alef.Nun.Yod (א.נ.י)

Moon's Seals

First Seal of the Moon
Cheit.Ayin.Mem (ח.ע.מ)
Peh.Vav.Yod (פ.ו.י)
Samech.Yod.Teit (ס.י.ט)
Lamed.Caf.Beit (ל.כ.ב)

Second Seal of the Moon
Yod.Zayin.Lamed (י.ז. ל)
Yod.Lamed.Yod (י.ל.י)
Lamed.Alef.Vav (ל.א.ו)
Alef.Yod.Ayin (א.י.ע)

Third Seal of the Moon
Yod.Zayin.Lamed (י.ז. ל)
Yod.Lamed.Yod (י.ל.י)
Nun.Lamed.Caf (נ.ל.ך)
Yod.Lamed.Hei (י.ל. ה)

Fourth Seal of the Moon
Caf.Hei.Tav (כ.ה.ת)
Lamed.Alef.Vav (ל.א.ו)
Yod.Yod.Yod (י.י.י)
Vav.Mem.Beit (ו.מ.ב)

Fifth Seal of the Moon
Lamed.Lamed.Hei (ל.ל. ה)
Hei.Reish.Yod (ה.ר.י)
Hei.Zain.Yod (ה.ז.י)
Mem.Yod.Caf (מ.י.כ)

Sixth Seal of the Moon
Samech.Alef.Lamed (ס.א.ל)
Hei.Kof.Mem (ה.ק.מ)
Reish.Hei.Ayin (ר.ה.ע)
Nun.Nun.Alef (נ.נ.א)

Mars' Seals

First Seal of Mars
Reish.Hei.Ayin (ר.ה.ע)
Vav.Vav.Lamed (ו.ו.ל)
Lamed.Caf.Beit (ל.כ.ב)
Mem.Beit.Hei (מ.ב. ה)

Second Seal of Mars.
Mem.Hei.Shin (מ.ה.ש)
Ayin.Lamed.Mem (ע.ל. ם).
Vav.Mem.Beit (ו.מ.ב)
Yod.Lamed.Yod (י.ל.י)

Third Seal of Mars.
Caf.Hei.Tav (כ.ה.ת)
Lamed.Alef.Vav (ל.א.ו)
Lamed.Vav.Vav (ל.ו.ו)
Lamed.Caf.Beit (ל.כ.ב)

Fourth Seal of Mars
Mem.Nun.Dalet (מ.נ.ד)
Lamed.Caf.Beit (ל.כ.ב)
Dalet.Nun.Yod (ד.נ.י)
Mem.Yod.Caf (מ.י.כ)

Fifth Seal of Mars
Yod.Lamed.Yod (י.ל.י)
Lamed.Alef.Vav (ל.א.ו).
Lamed.Vav.Vav (ל.ו.ו)
Yod.Yod.Yod (י.י.י)

Sixth Seal of Mars
Yod.Lamed.Yod (י.ל.י)
Lamed.Caf.Beit (ל.כ.ב)
Cheit.Ayin.Mem (ח.ע.מ)
Hei.Yod.Yod (ה.י.י)

Seventh Seal of Mars
Alef.Yod.Ayin (א.י.ע)
Reish.Alef.Hei (ר.א. ה)
Cheit.Ayin.Mem (ח.ע.מ)
Lamed.Alef.Vav (ל.א.ו)

Mercury's Seals

First Seal of Mercury
Caf.Vav.Kof (כ.ו.ק)
Shin.Alef.Hei (ש.א. ה)
Reish.Hei.Ayin (ר.ה.ע)
Mem.Yod.Hei (מ.י. ה)

Second Seal of Mercury
Samech.Yod.Teit (ס.י.ט)
Vav.Hei.Vav (ו.ה.ו)
Nun.Tav.Hei (נ.ת. ה)
Vav.Shin.Reish (ו.ש.ר)

Third Seal of Mercury
Hei.Zain.Yod (ה.ז.י)
Ayin.Lamed.Mem (ע.ל.מ).
Mem.Lamed.Hei (מ.ל. ה)
Yod.Yod.Zayin (י.י.ז)

Fourth Seal of Mercury
Hei.Reish.Yod (ה.ר.י)
Nun.Tav.Hei (נ.ת. ה)
Reish.Yod.Yod (ר.י.י)
Mem.Cheit.Yod (מ.ח.י)

Fifth Seal of Mercury
Samech.Alef.Lamed (ס.א.ל)
Lamed.Caf.Beit (ל.כ.ב)
Reish.Hei.Ayin (ר.ה.ע)
Yod.Reish.Tav (י.ר.ת)

Jupiter's Seals

First Seal of Jupiter
Samech.Alef.Lamed (ס.א.ל)
Caf.Hei.Tav (כ.ה.ת)
Vav.Vav.Lamed (ו.ו.ל)
Reish.Hei.Ayin (ר.ה.ע)

Second Seal of Jupiter
Mem.Hei.Shin (מ.ה.ש)
Caf.Hei.Tav (כ.ה.ת)
Alef.Lamed.Dalet (א.ל.ד)
Lamed.Alef.Vav (ל.א.ו)

Third Seal of Jupiter
Yod.Yod.Yod (י.י.י)
Caf.Hei.Tav (כ.ה.ת)
Alef.Lamed.Dalet (א.ל.ד)
Lamed.Alef.Vav (ל.א.ו)

Fourth Seal of Jupiter
Samech.Alef.Lamed (ס.א.ל)
Yod.Reish.Tav (י.ר.ת)
Vav.Hei.Vav (ו.ה.ו)
Alef.Lamed.Dalet (א.ל.ד)

Fifth Seal of Jupiter
Hei.Reish.Yod (ה.ר.י)
Shin.Alef.Hei (ש.א.ה)
Reish.Alef.Hei (ר.א.ה)
Hei.Zain.Yod (ה.ז.י)

Sixth Seal of Jupiter
Yod.Lamed.Hei (י.ל.ה)
Yod.Yod.Yod (י.י.י)
Mem.Nun.Dalet (מ.נ.ד)
Lamed.Caf.Beit (ל.כ.ב)

Seventh Seal of Jupiter
Lamed.Alef.Vav (ל.א.ו)
Cheit.Hei.Vav (ח.ה.ו)
Nun.Lamed.Caf (נ.ל.ך)
Alef.Nun.Yod (א.נ.י)

Venus' Seals

First Seal of Venus
Ayin.Lamed.Mem (ע.ל.מ)
Mem.Hei.Shin (מ.ה.ש)
Caf.Vav.Kof (כ.ו.ק)
Samech.Yod.Teit – (ס.י.ט)

Second Seal of Venus
Alef.Caf.Alef (א.כ.א)
Caf.Lamed.Yod (כ.ל.י)
Lamed.Hei.Cheit (ל.ה.ח)
Mem.Tzadi.Reish (מ.צ.ר)

Third Seal of Venus
Nun.Tav.Hei (נ.ת.ה)
Lamed.Caf.Beit (ל.כ.ב)
Samech.Alef.Lamed (ס.א.ל)
Caf.Vav.Kof (כ.ו.ק)

Fourth Seal of Venus
Alef.Caf.Alef (א.כ.א)
Mem.Beit.Hei (מ.ב.ה)
Cheit.Beit.Vav (ח.ב.ו)
Mem.Yod.Hei (מ.י.ה)

Fifth Seal of Venus
Lamed.Vav.Vav (ל.ו.ו)
Mem.Lamed.Hei (מ.ל.ה)
Ayin.Mem.Mem (ע.מ.ם)
Hei.Reish.Yod (ה.ר.י)

Saturn's Seals

First Seal of Saturn
Hei.Zain.Yod (ה.ז.י)
Yod.Yod.Zayin (י.י.ז)
Mem.Lamed.Hei (מ.ל.ה)
Mem.Beit.Hei (מ.ב.ה)

Second Seal of Saturn
Samech.Alef.Lamed (ס.א.ל)
Samech.Yod.Teit (ס.י.ט)
Mem.Lamed.Hei (מ.ל.ה)
Mem.Cheit.Yod (מ.ח.י)

Third Seal of Saturn
Alef.Lamed.Dalet (א.ל.ד)
Lamed.Alef.Vav (ל.א.ו)
Reish.Yod.Yod (ר.י.י)
Cheit.Ayin.Mem (ח.ע.ם)

Fourth Seal of Saturn
Hei.Reish.Yod (ה.ר.י)
Mem.Yod.Hei (מ.י.ה)
Samech.Alef.Lamed (ס.א.ל)
Vav.Vav.Lamed (ו.ו.ל)

Fifth Seal of Saturn
Lamed.Alef.Vav (ל.א.ו)
Alef.Lamed.Dalet (א.ל.ד)
Hei.Hei.Ayin (ה.ה.ע)
Mem.Nun.Kof (מ.נ.ק)

Sixth Seal of Saturn
Yod.Lamed.Hei (י.ל.ה)
Peh.Vav.Yod (פ.ו.י)
Yod.Lamed.Yod (י.ל.י)
Caf.Hei.Tav (כ.ה.ת)

Seventh Seal of Saturn
Mem.Lamed.Hei (מ.ל.ה)
Yod.Reish.Tav (י.ר.ת)
Nun.Nun.Alef (נ.נ.א)
Mem.Beit.Hei (מ.ב.ה)

Summary Attunement and Activation of King Solomon's Seals

1st. Seal of The Sun: *Magic and control over all beings. Will make you shine with Divine Light and get all your desires and wishes fulfilled. Provides protection from any harm or danger. The face on this seal is of Archangel Metatron.*
'Behold His face and form by Whom all things were made, and Whom all creatures obey'
'Oh Mighty EL-Shaddai the most powerful God, I ask you to five me control over all beings. Do so by the merit of the great King Solomon'.
Feel connection with the Seal, then say:
'In gratitude I come before You, El-Shaddai, the great controller of the man and beast. I know that You will grant this wish for me through this holy Talisman of the great King Solomon. Amen'.
Attunement (First Time): 'In the Name of Father and Mother Divine, I receive the attunement to the First Seal of the Sun'. 'The Creator makes my wishes come true'.
Names of God for Attunement: Yod.Hei.Hei (י.ה.ה), Mem.Lamed.Hei (מ.ל.ה), Lamed.Vav.Vav (ל.ו.ו), Yod.Beit.Mem (י.ב.מ)
Activation (After First Time): 'In the Names of Father and Mother Divine, and of the Great King Solomon, I activate the First Seal of the Sun'.

2nd. Seal of The Sun: *Makes your enemies surrender to you. Represses the arrogance and pride of those who stand between you and your aspirations and will make them surrender and fulfill all your requests.*
'I invoke the Angels:
<u>Shemeshiel,</u> who bears the knowledge and power of the Sun.
<u>Paimoniah,</u> who will humble individuals before me.
<u>Rekhodiah,</u> who is very powerful in subjugating individuals to my will.
<u>Malkhiel,</u> who grants blessings, boons and bestows healings. Feel connection with the Seal.
Attunement (First Time): 'In the Name of Father and Mother Divine, I receive the attunement to the Second Seal of the Sun'. 'The Creator protects me from enemies and evil plans'.
Names of God for Attunement: Cheit.Hei.Vav (ח.ה.ו), Vav.Vav.Lamed (ו.ו.ל), Mem.Tzadi.Reish (מ.צ.ר), Alef.Yod.Ayin (א.י.ע)
Activation (After First Time): 'In the Names of Father and Mother Divine, and of the Great King Solomon, I activate the Second Seal of the Sun'.

3rd. Seal of The Sun: *Fame, fortune and fulfilment of wishes. Empowers you with control and respect, attracts fame and fortune, success and fulfillment of wishes.*
'My Kingdom is an everlasting Kingdom, and my dominion endures from age to age' (Psalm 145: 13).
'Oh Mighty YHVH, the most powerful Name, I ask You to bless me with wealth, more than I will ever need. Do so by the merit of the great King Solomon'. Feel connection with the Seal, then say:
'In gratitude, I come before You YHVH, the Great Provider. I know that You will grant this request for me through this holy Talisman of the great King Solomon'.
Attunement (First Time): 'In the Name of Father and Mother Divine, I receive the attunement to the Third Seal of the Sun'. 'The Creator helps me to achieve success in my life'.
Names of God for Attunement: Samech.Alef.Lamed (ס.א.ל), Nun.Nun.Alef (נ.נ.א), Ayin.Nun.Vav (ע.נ.ו), Yod.Beit.Mem (י.ב.מ)
Activation (After First Time): 'In the Names of Father and Mother Divine, and of the Great King Solomon, I activate the Third Seal of the Sun'.

4th. Seal of The Sun: *Lets you see the spirits at work. Allows you to look into the soul of another person and see beyond their external impression. This Pentacle aids in enhancing empathy and understanding towards others, while simultaneously diminishing the influence of one's ego.*
'Consider and hear me, O Lord my God; Enlighten my eyes, lest I sleep the sleep of death; lest my eneny say: I have prevailed against him' (Psalm 13: 3,4).
Feel connection with the Seal.
Attunement (First Time): 'In the Name of Father and Mother Divine, I receive the attunement to the Fourth Seal of the Sun'. 'The Creator helps me to channel higher energies'.
Names of God for Attunement: Ayin.Shin.Lamed (ע.ש.ל), Mem.Cheit.Yod (מ.ח.י), Reish.Alef.Hei (ר.א.ה), Nun.Tav.Hei (נ.ת.ה)
Activation (After First Time): 'In the Names of Father and Mother Divine, and of the Great King Solomon, I activate the Fourth Seal of the Sun'.

5th. Seal of The Sun: *Supernatural transportability. Will help you develop mystical powers and open your eyes to foresee the possible dangers from harmful spirits and use their power to your advantage.*
'He shall give His Angels charge over you, to keep you in all your ways. They shall bear you up in their hands' (Psalm 91:11,12).
Feel connection with the Seal, then say:
'In the Names of Father and Mother Divine, and of the Great King Solomon, May my travels be safe and swift. Amen'.
Attunement (First Time): 'In the Name of Father and Mother Divine, I receive the attunement to the Fifth Seal of the Sun'. 'The Creator improves my creativity'.
Names of God for Attunement: Hei.Reish.Yod (ה.ר.י), Yod.Reish.Tav (י.ר.ת), Lamed.Alef.Vav (ל.א.ו), Hei.Zain.Yod (ה.ז.י)
Activation (After First Time): 'In the Names of Father and Mother Divine, and of the Great King Solomon, I activate the Fifth Seal of the Sun'.

6th. Seal of The Sun: *Power of invisibility. Will help you become invisible and disappear from the people around you. Also helps to amend your personal integrity.*

'Make their eyes dark so that they do not see; and let their loins tremble continually' (Psalm 69:24).
'They have eyes, but they do not see' (Psalm 135:16).
Feel connection with the Seal, then say:
'May I disappear to the sight of man and beast. Amen'
Attunement (First Time): 'In the Name of Father and Mother Divine, I receive the attunement to the Sixth Seal of the Sun. The Creator helps me to become invisible to those I wish not to see me.
Names of God for Attunement: Yod.Zayin.Lamed (י.ז.ל), Peh.Vav.Yod (פ.ו.י), Hei.Reish.Yod (ה.ר.י), Lamed.Vav.Vav (ל.ו.ו)
Activation (After First Time): 'In the Names of Father and Mother Divine, and of the Great King Solomon, I activate the Sixth Seal of the Sun'.

7th. Seal of The Sun: *Release from addictions. Releases internal and external influences that bind you, blockages, binding to people, dependency on negative desires or addictions and opens the way to success.*

'You have loosed my bonds. I will offer to You the sacrifice of thanksgiving. And will call upon the Name of the Lord' (Psalm 116: 16, 17).
Feel connection with the Seal, then say:
'I invoke the Seraphim, the Cherubim, and the Angels Ariel, Tharsis, Chasan, Arel, Phorlakh and Taliahad. Go you of the great angelic orders, go and do my bidding and unbind me in the name of the great King Solomon. Amen'.
Attunement (First Time): 'In the Name of Father and Mother Divine, I receive the attunement to the Seventh Seal of the Sun. Thanks to the Creator, I am free from any prison'.
Names of God for Attunement: Vav.Hei.Vav (ו.ה.ו), Peh.Hei.Lamed (פ.ה.ל), Lamed.Hei.Cheit (ל.ה.ח), Alef.Nun.Yod (א.נ.י)
Activation (After First Time): 'In the Names of Father and Mother Divine, and of the Great King Solomon, I activate the Seventh Seal of the Sun'.

1st. Seal of the Moon: *Opens doors to success, cancels spells. Opens all doors and locks, releases any blockages, barriers, evil eye or spells and bring you to a new path of success.*

'He has broken the gates of brass and smitten the bars of iron in sunder' (Psalm 107:16).
'I invoke the angels: Schioel, Vaol, Yashiel and Vehiel'.
Feel connection with the Seal, then say:
'Go you angels of this mighty seal, go and fulfill my request and guide me in the name of the great King Solomon. Amen'.
Attunement (First Time): 'In the Name of Father and Mother Divine, I receive the attunement to the 1st. Seal of the Moon'. 'Now my vision is clear, and the doors are open'.
Names of God for Attunement: Cheit.Ayin.Mem (ח.ע.ם), Peh.Vav.Yod (פ.ו.י), Samech.Yod.Teit – (ס.י.ט), Lamed.Caf.Beit (ל.כ.ב)
Activation (After First Time): 'In the Names of Father and Mother Divine, and of the Great King Solomon, I activate the 1st. Seal of the Moon'.

2nd. Seal of the Moon: *Protection from natural disasters. Protection from natural disasters, sea storms, earthquakes and lightning, storms at travel and sailing.*

'In Elohim have I put my trust, I will not fear, what can man do unto me? (Psalm 56:11-13).
'Oh protector angel Abariel I ask you in the name of the great King Solomon, you protect us from all of nature's whims. Be my protector'.
Feel connection with the Seal, then say:
'By this great seal shall it be so'.
Attunement (First Time): 'In the Name of Father and Mother Divine, I receive the attunement to the 2nd. Seal of the Moon'. 'I invoke the Creator's power to protect me from any calamity'.
Names of God for Attunement: Yod.Zayin.Lamed (י.ז.ל), Yod.Lamed.Yod (י.ל.י), Lamed.Alef.Vav (ל.א.ו), Alef.Yod.Ayin (א.י.ע)
Activation (After First Time): 'In the Names of Father and Mother Divine, and of the Great King Solomon, I activate the 2nd. Seal of the Moon'.

3rd. Seal of the Moon: *Protection from poltergeists and hauntings. Protection from natural disasters, sea storms, earthquakes and lightning, storms at travel and sailing.*

'Be pleased O God to deliver me, O God make haste to help me' (Psalm 40:13).
'I invoke the angels Aub and Vevaphel to protect me from all spirits that wish to harm me, or my loved ones. By this great seal shall it be so'.
Feel connection with the Seal, then say:
'Oh great angels go forth in front of me and protect me and my loved ones, from the evils that have come from the other side. Amen'.
Attunement (First Time): 'In the Name of Father and Mother Divine, I receive the attunement to the 3rd. Seal of the Moon. 'I invoke the power of the Creator to protect me from any danger'.
Names of God for Attunement: Yod.Zayin.Lamed (י.ז.ל), Yod.Lamed.Yod (י.ל.י), Nun.Lamed.Caf (נ.ל.ך), Yod.Lamed.Hei (י.ל.ה)
Activation (After First Time): 'In the Names of Father and Mother Divine, and of the Great King Solomon, I activate the 3rd. Seal of the Moon'.

4th. Seal of the Moon: *Defends from evil and teaches about crystals and herbs. Guards the body and mind from any harm and injury.*

'Let them be confounded who persecute me and let me not be confounded; let them fear and not I' (Psalm 35:4). 'Oh great God Eheieh Asher Eheieh, that is the Name you said unto Moses, your faithful servant. Teach unto me the secrets of the powers of nature. May the stones and plants whisper their secrets in my soul'.

Feel connection with the Seal, then say:

'I now invoke the angels Yahel and Sofiel to teach me the wonderful works of nature and the properties therein. By this great seal shall it be so'.

Attunement (First Time): 'In the Name of Father and Mother Divine, I receive the attunement to the 4th Seal of the Moon'. 'I invoke the power of the Creator to protect me from any injury and to give me the wisdom of nature'.

Names of God for Attunement: Caf.Hei.Tav (כ.ה.ת), Lamed.Alef.Vav (ל.א.ו), Yod.Yod.Yod (י.י.י), Vav.Mem.Beit (ו.מ.ב)

Activation (After First Time): 'In the Names of Father and Mother Divine, and of the Great King Solomon, I activate the 4th. Seal of the Moon'.

5th. Seal of the Moon: *Protection during sleep and answers in dreams. Strengthens the spirit as it ascends to higher realms during sleep, guards from evil spirits and nightmares, provides deep sleep and clear insights from dreams.*

'May God rise and His enemies be scattered; that those who hate Him may flee before Him' (Psalm 68:1). 'Oh, great God YHVH-ELOHIM, that is the Name You revealed to Jacob, who had visions in his sleep. I ask that I too will be recipient of great visions in my sleep. By this seal shall it be so'.

Feel connection with the Seal, then say:

'I now invoke the angels Iachadiel and Azarel to protect me at night from spirits that lie, and to reveal me what I need to know, during my sleep. By this seal of the great King Solomon shall it be so'.

Attunement (First Time): 'In the Name of Father and Mother Divine, I receive the attunement to the 5th. Seal of the Moon'. 'I invoke the power of the Creator to protect my sleep and to give me understanding of my dreams'.

Names of God for Attunement: Lamed.Lamed.Hei (ל.ל.ה), Hei.Reish.Yod (ה.ר.י), Hei.Zain.Yod (ה.ז.י), Mem.Yod.Caf (מ.י.כ)

Activation (After First Time): 'In the Names of Father and Mother Divine, and of the Great King Solomon, I activate the 5th. Seal of the Moon'.

6th. Seal of the Moon: *Brings rain, controls the weather. Carries the gracefulness of water, showering blessed rains, and guards against drought, hunger and poverty.*

'All the fountains of the great depth were broken...And the rain fell upon the earth' (Genesis 7:11-12).

Feel connection with the Seal, then say:

'By the great power of the Moon, I will control the weather as did the Great and Mighty King Solomon'.

Attunement (First Time): 'In the Name of Father and Mother Divine, I receive the attunement to the 6th. Seal of the Moon'. 'I invoke the power of the Creator to remove famine and rain abundance within me'.

Names of God for Attunement: Samech.Alef.Lamed (ס.א.ל), Hei.Kof.Mem (ה.ק.ם), Reish.Hei.Ayin (ר.ה.ע), Nun.Nun.Alef (נ.נ.א)

Activation (After First Time): 'In the Names of Father and Mother Divine, and of the Great King Solomon, I activate the 6th. Seal of the Moon'.

1st. Seal of Mars: *Passion to succeed in chosen path. Will enhance courage, enthusiasm, ambition and passion for your occupation to succeed in your chosen path.*

'I invoke the angels: Madimiel, Bartzachiah, Eschiel, and Ithuriel'.

Feel connection with the Seal, then say:

'Go you angels of this mighty seal, go and fulfill my request and guide me in the name of the great King Solomon. Amen'.

Attunement (First Time): 'In the Name of Father and Mother Divine, I receive the attunement to the 1st. Seal of Mars'. 'I am grateful to the Creator for the courage He gives me. All the inhibitions, fears, and restraints that have held me back are dissolving'.

Names of God for Attunement: Reish.Hei.Ayin (ר.ה.ע), Vav.Vav.Lamed (ו.ו.ל), Lamed.Caf.Beit (ל.כ.ב), Mem.Beit.Hei (מ.ב.ה)

Activation (After First Time): 'In the Names of Father and Mother Divine, and of the Great King Solomon, I activate the 1st. Seal of Mars'.

2nd. Seal of Mars: *Heals diseases, pain and injuries. Heals all kinds of diseases, pain and injuries. The seal should be applied unto the afflicted area of the body.*

'In Him was life, and the life was the light of man' (John 1:4).

Feel connection with the Seal, then say:

'In gratitude I come before You, Yahweh-Elohim of the universe, I know that you will grant this wish for me through this holy Talisman of the great King Solomon'.

Attunement (First Time): 'In the Name of Father and Mother Divine, I receive the attunement to the 2nd. Seal of Mars'. 'I invoke the power of the Creator to heal my body, mind, and spirit. Healing energy fills all of my organs, body and soul that are fully functioning'.

Names of God for Attunement: Mem.Hei.Shin (מ.ה.ש), Ayin.Lamed.Mem (ע.ל.ם), Vav.Mem.Beit (ו.מ.ב), Yod.Lamed.Yod (י.ל.י)

Activation (After First Time): 'In the Names of Father and Mother Divine, and of the Great King Solomon, I activate the 2nd. Seal of Mars'.

3rd. Seal of Mars: *Success in negotiations. Helps you overcome your opponents and subdue resistance, bring success in negotiations and conflict resolution.*

'Who is so great a God as our God? (Psalm 77:13).
Feel connection with the Seal, then say:
'In gratitude I come before You, El-Shaddai-Eloha of the Universe.
I know that You will grant this wish for me through this holy Talisman of the great King Solomon'.
Attunement (First Time): 'In the Name of Father and Mother Divine, I receive the attunement to the 3rd. Seal of Mars'. 'Negative people and situations that oppose me vanish and have no influence on me. I am guarded and protected by the Creator of all'.
Names of God for Attunement: Caf.Hei.Tav (כ.ה.ת), Lamed.Alef.Vav (ל.א.ו), Lamed.Vav.Vav (ל.ו.ו), Lamed.Caf.Beit (ל.כ.ב)
Activation (After First Time): 'In the Names of Father and Mother Divine, and of the Great King Solomon, I activate the 3rd. Seal of Mars'.

4th. Seal of Mars: *Victory in competitions. Victory in a any argument or competition, gives courage and power in trials and quarrels, and supports good decision-making.*

'The Lord at your right hand shall wound even Kings in the day of His wrath' (Psalm 110:5).
Feel connection with the Seal, then say:
'In gratitude I come before you Agla-Adonai-El, of the Universe. I know that you will grant this wish for me through this holy Talisman of the great King Solomon'.
Attunement (First Time): 'In the Name of Father and Mother Divine, I receive the attunement to the 4th. Seal of Mars'. 'I transcend my weaknesses, while my inner strength increases. I am filled with love and self-confidence'.
Names of God for Attunement: Mem.Nun.Dalet (מ.נ.ד), Lamed.Caf.Beit (ל.כ.ב), Dalet.Nun.Yod (ד.נ.י), Mem.Yod.Caf (מ.י.כ)
Activation (After First Time): 'In the Names of Father and Mother Divine, and of the Great King Solomon, I activate the 4th. Seal of Mars'.

5th. Seal of Mars: *Magic powers and protection. Gives you magical and spiritual powers and helps you control evil and dark forces.*

'You shall go upon the lion and adder, the young lion and the dragon shall you tread under your feet' (Psalm 91:13).
Feel connection with the Seal, then say:
'In gratitude I come before You, King of the Universe,
I know that You will grant this wish for me through this Holy Talisman of the great King Solomon'.
Attunement (First Time): 'In the Name of Father and Mother Divine, I receive the attunement to the 5th. Seal of Mars'. 'My negative thoughts are cleansed, despair, frustration, and sadness leave. I am protected from the harmful forces that try to harm me, and from all dangers and decrees. The Creator protects me through his angels'.
Names of God for Attunement: Yod.Lamed.Yod (י.ל.י), Lamed.Alef.Vav (ל.א.ו), Lamed.Vav.Vav (ל.ו.ו), Yod.Yod.Yod (י.י.י)
Activation (After First Time): 'In the Names of Father and Mother Divine, and of the Great King Solomon, I activate the 5th. Seal of Mars'.

6th. Seal of Mars: *Turns opponents' weapons against them. Protects against harm and threat and causes your opponent's own weapons to turn against him.*

'His sword shall enter into his own heart, and his bows shall be broken' (Psalm 37:15).
Feel connection with the Seal, then say:
'In gratitude I come before You, Yahweh the great protector of the universe.
I know that You will grant this wish for me through this holy Talisman of the great King Solomon'.
Attunement (First Time): 'In the Name of Father and Mother Divine, I receive the attunement to the 6th. Seal of Mars'. 'Enemies, adversaries and negative presences disappear from my life. Nothing hinders or prevents me from achieving my goals'.
Names of God for Attunement: Yod.Lamed.Yod (י.ל.י), Lamed.Caf.Beit (ל.כ.ב), Cheit.Ayin.Mem (ח.ע.ם), Hei.Yod.Yod (ה.י.י)
Activation (After First Time): 'In the Names of Father and Mother Divine, and of the Great King Solomon, I activate the 6th. Seal of Mars'.

7th. Seal of Mars: *Confuses and blinds your adversaries. Gives you the ability to confuse your adversaries and blind their vision so they can not harm you.*

'He gave them hail for rain and flaming fire in their land. He smote their vines also, and their fig-trees' (Psalm 105:32).
Feel connection with the Seal, then say:
'In gratitude I come before You El-Yee-Ya, the great controller of the tempests. I know that You will grant this request for me through this holy Talisman of the great King Solomon'.
Attunement (First Time): 'In the Name of Father and Mother Divine, I receive the attunement to the 7th. Seal of Mars'. The light of the Creator protects me from anyone who wants to hurt me. The forces of evil cannot approach me, any curse or occult attack vanishes in the light of the Creator.
Names of God for Attunement: Alef.Yod.Ayin (א.י.ע), Reish.Alef.Hei (ר.א.ה), Cheit.Ayin.Mem (ח.ע.ם), Lamed.Alef.Vav (ל.א.ו)
Activation (After First Time): 'In the Names of Father and Mother Divine, and of the Great King Solomon, I activate the 7th. Seal of Mars'.

1st. Seal of Mercury: *Personal magnetism. Gives personal charm and charisma and magnetize people to you. Good for attracting a soul mate or for any social purpose.*

'I invoke the angels Yekahel and Agiel. Make me irresistible to the people I encounter, and make me mentally strong, so I may appreciate my power. Amen'.

Feel connection with the Seal, then say:

'In gratitude I thank you, Oh mighty angels. I know that you will grant this wish for me through this holy Talisman of the great King Solomon'.

Attunement (First Time): 'In the Name of Father and Mother Divine, I receive the attunement to the 1st. Seal of Mercury'. 'I am grateful to the Creator for the charm he gives me. I now express my divine beauty'.

Names of God for Attunement: Caf.Vav.Kof (ק.ו.כ), Shin.Alef.Hei (ה.א.ש), Reish.Hei.Ayin (ע.ה.ר), Mem.Yod.Hei (ה.י.מ)

Activation (After First Time): 'In the Names of Father and Mother Divine, and of the Great King Solomon, I activate the 1st. Seal of Mercury'.

2nd. Seal of Mercury: *Attain the impossible. Helps you attain the impossible and fulfill your wishes even when they are contrary to the laws of nature.*

'I invoke the angel Boel, who commands the four corners of the Earth. By the power of this great seal of the great King Solomon, I implore you to help me remedy this pressing issue. Amen'.

Feel connection with the Seal, then say:

'In gratitude I thank you Boel. I know that you will grant this wish for me through this holy Talisman of the great King Solomon'.

Attunement (First Time): 'In the Name of Father and Mother Divine, I receive the attunement to the 2nd. Seal of Mercury'. 'I invoke the Creator's power to make me fertile so that I can accomplish what I desire'.

Names of God for Attunment: Samech.Yod.Teit – (ט.י.ס), Vav.Hei.Vav (ו.ה.ו), Nun.Tav.Hei (ה.ת.נ), Vav.Shin.Reish (ר.ש.ו)

Activation (After First Time): 'In the Names of Father and Mother Divine, and of the Great King Solomon, I activate the 2nd. Seal of Mercury'.

3rd. Seal of Mercury: *Influence with words. Enhances the eloquence and expressional skills and helps you influence people with your written or verbal words.*

'I invoke the angels: Kokaviel, Gheoriah, Savaniah and Hokmahiel to give me the power to learn and write with ease and great creativity, so that I can gain the love and admiration of others through my work. Amen'.

Feel connection with the Seal, then say:

'Go you angels of this mighty seal, go and fulfill my request and guide me in the name of the great King Solomon. Amen'.

Attunement (First Time): 'In the Name of Father and Mother Divine, I receive the attunement to the 3rd. Seal of Mercury'. 'By the Creator's will I now express all my creativity'

Names of God for Attunement: Hei.Zain.Yod (י.ז.ה), Ayin.Lamed.Mem (מ.ל.ע), Mem.Lamed.Hei (ה.ל.מ), Yod.Yod.Zayin (ז.י.י)

Activation (After First Time): 'In the Names of Father and Mother Divine, and of the Great King Solomon, I activate the 3rd. Seal of Mercury'.

4th. Seal of Mercury: *Wisdom and knowledge. Will help you acquire wisdom, know and understand the thoughts of others and narrow the gaps between you and your loved ones.*

'Wisdom and virtue are in his house, and the knowledge of all things remains with him forever' (Psalm 112:3). 'God, fix Thou the volatile, and let there be unto the void restriction'. 'I invoke the Name of God: EL, the Mighty God of creation. He who has brought forth knowledge of all kinds. Bless me by the merits of this great seal of the Great King Solomon with the knowledge and wisdom I require'

Feel connection with the Seal, then say:

'Thank You El, for You Are the granter of all knowledge'.

Attunement (First Time): 'In the Name of Father and Mother Divine, I receive the attunement to the 4th. Seal of Mercury'. 'Divine wisdom now shines through me'.

Names of God for Attunement: Hei.Reish.Yod (י.ר.ה), Nun.Tav.Hei (ה.ת.נ), Reish.Yod.Yod (י.י.ר), Mem.Cheit.Yod (י.ח.מ)

Activation (After First Time): 'In the Names of Father and Mother Divine, and of the Great King Solomon, I activate the 4th. Seal of Mercury'.

5th. Seal of Mercury: *Opens doors and portals (spiritual and physical). Breaks all blockages and barriers, overcomes resistance, or defeatism and opens the door to success.*

'Lift up your heads, you gate; lift them up, you ancient doors, that the King of glory may come in' (Psalm 24:9). 'I invoke the Name of God: YHVH-EL, the mighty God of Creation, and Father of us all, He who has no barrier. Bless me by the merits of this great seal of Your servant King Solomon with the ability to open and enter spiritual portals that have been closed to those who are uninitiated. Amen'.

Feel connection with the Seal, then say:

'Thank You YHVH-EL our Father, for You Are the Guardian of all knowledge and dimensions'.

Attunement (First Time): 'In the Name of Father and Mother Divine, I receive the attunement to the 5th. Seal of Mercury'. 'All doors are now open to me and obstacles are removed'.

Names of God for Attunement: Samech.Alef.Lamed (ל.א.ס), Lamed.Caf.Beit (ב.כ.ל), Reish.Hei.Ayin (ע.ה.ר), Yod.Reish.Tav (ת.ר.י)

Activation (After First Time): 'In the Names of Father and Mother Divine, and of the Great King Solomon, I activate the 5th. Seal of Mercury'.

1st. Seal of Jupiter: *Success and financial abundance. Places you on a new path of success, attracts abundance and good livelihood, richness and material gain.*

'I invoke the Angels: Netoniel (fame), Devachiah (equilibrium and peace), Tzedeqiah (riches, glory and honour), and Parasiel (great treasures).'
Feel connection with the Seal, then say:
'Go you angels of this mighty seal, go and bring forth abundance in the name of the great King Solomon. Amen'.
Attunement (First Time): 'In the Name of Father and Mother Divine, I receive the attunement to the 1st.Seal of Jupiter'. 'My life enters a path of manifestation of abundance, and I am ready to receive it. I let go of everything I don't need any more to make room for abundance'.
Names of God for Attunement: Samech.Alef.Lamed (ס.א.ל), Caf.Hei.Tav (כ.ה.ת), Vav.Vav.Lamed (ו.ו.ל), Reish.Hei.Ayin (ר.ה.ע).
Activation (After First Time): 'In the Names of Father and Mother Divine, and of the Great King Solomon, I activate the 1st.Seal of Jupiter'.

2nd. Seal of Jupiter: *Glory and peace of mind. Helps to acquire glory, dignity and tranquillity, induces balance of body and mind.*

'Well-being and riches are in his house, and his righteousness endures forever' (Psalm 112:3).
Feel connection with the Seal, then say:
'In gratitude I come before You Yahweh-Ehieh, with Your power I attract wealth and success to me. You are my Father, the great Lord and Father of all there is. I know You will bring me the prosperity that I request through this holy Talisman of Solomon Your servant'.
Attunement (First Time): 'In the Name of Father and Mother Divine, I receive the attunement to the 2nd. Seal of Jupiter'. I am worthy of receiving abundance from the universe effortlessly and the divine loving light rebalances me and purifies me.
Names of God for Attunement: Mem.Hei.Shin (מ.ה.ש), Caf.Hei.Tav (כ.ה.ת), Alef.Lamed.Dalet (א.ל.ד), Lamed.Alef.Vav (ל.א.ו).
Activation (After First Time): 'In the Names of Father and Mother Divine, and of the Great King Solomon, I activate the 2nd. Seal of Jupiter'.

3rd. Seal of Jupiter: *Clears and protects houses. Defends and protects against opponents and evil spirits, curses and spells in the house and around it.*

'They that trust in the LORD shall be as Mount Zion, which cannot be removed, but abides forever' (Psalm 125:1)
Feel connection with the Seal, then say:
'In gratitude I come before You, Yahweh-Adonai, the great protector and implore You to protect me from the spirits and entities that wish to harm me, by the power vested in this seal, You will protect me. Amen'.
Attunement (First Time): 'In the Name of Father and Mother Divine, I receive the attunement to the 3rd..Seal of Jupiter'.
The Creator protects me from all harmful forces and evil spirits. All negative forces disappear from my life.
Names of God for Attunement: Yod.Yod.Yod (י.י.י), Caf.Hei.Tav (כ.ה.ת), Alef.Lamed.Dalet (א.ל.ד), Lamed.Alef.Vav (ל.א.ו).
Activation (After First Time): 'In the Names of Father and Mother Divine, and of the Great King Solomon, I activate the 3rd.Seal of Jupiter'.

4th. Seal of Jupiter: *Great financial abundance. Helps to enjoy the best treasures of life, comfort and honour, enrichment with abundance and good harvest.*

'Wealth and riches are in His house, and His righteousness endures forever' (Psalm 112:3).
'I invoke the angels: Adoniel (who increases luck in all financial matters) and Bariel (the giver of long life and health)
Feel connection with the Seal, then say:
'In gratitude I come before angels Adoniel and Bariel for listening to my request,
in the name of the great King Solomon and God Almighty you will grant this request for me'.
Attunement (First Time): 'In the Name of Father and Mother Divine, I receive the attunement to the 4th.Seal of Jupiter'.
'I am blessed by the abundance of the Creator; his light floods me. I let go of doubts, fears, and concerns about my sustenance in front of the Creator who dissolves them'.
Names of God for Attunement: Samech.Alef.Lamed (ס.א.ל), Yod.Reish.Tav (י.ר.ת), Vav.Hei.Vav (ו.ה.ו), Alef.Lamed.Dalet (א.ל.ד).
Activation (After First Time): 'In the Names of Father and Mother Divine, and of the Great King Solomon, I activate the 4th.Seal of Jupiter'.

5th. Seal of Jupiter: *Spiritual and psychic powers. To remove the veils from knowledge, revel Divine secrets, gain spiritual and psychic powers and fulfill your visions and dreams.*

'While I was among the exiles by the Kebar River, the heavens were opened, and I saw visions of God' (Ezekiel 1:1).
Feel connection with the Seal.
Attunement (First Time): 'In the Name of Father and Mother Divine, I receive the attunement to the 5th.Seal of Jupiter'. 'I climb the stair of my spiritual evolution, my eyes open, angels and sacred entities are revealed to me and guide me. I see beyond all illusions'.
Names of God for Attunement: Hei.Reish.Yod (ה.ר.י), Shin.Alef.Hei (ש.א.ה), Reish.Alef.Hei (ר.א.ה), Hei.Zain.Yod (ה.ז.י).
Activation (After First Time): 'In the Names of Father and Mother Divine, and of the Great King Solomon, I activate the 5th.Seal of Jupiter'.

6th. Seal of Jupiter: *Protection from earthly dangers. Provides protection against all earthly dangers, accidents and injury, keeps perils away wherever you go.*

'They have pierced my hands and my feet. I can count all my bones' (Psalm 22:16-17).

'I invoke the Seraphim, the Cherubim, the angels Ariel and Tharsis, to protect me in all my ways, in the name of the great King Solomon'.

Feel connection with the Seal.

'Go you of the great angelic orders, go and do my bidding, protect me from all harm in the name of the great King Solomon. Amen'.

Attunement (First Time): 'In the Name of Father and Mother Divine, I receive the attunement to the 6th.Seal of Jupiter'.'Any harmful power, every person, word, or negative act cannot hurt me. I release all the fears and anxieties of my life, I am full of courage and values'.

Names of God for Attunement: Yod.Lamed.Hei (י.ל.ה), Yod.Yod.Yod (י.י.י), Mem.Nun.Dalet (מ.נ.ד), Lamed.Caf.Beit (ל.כ.ב)

Activation (After First Time): 'In the Names of Father and Mother Divine, and of the Great King Solomon, I activate the 6th.Seal of Jupiter'.

7th. Seal of Jupiter: *Power over those who attempt to fail you. Has great power against poverty, famine, loss of property and people who attempt to fail you.*

'Raise the poor from the mire and bring the needy from the dunghill, to sit with the princes of his people' (Psalm 113:7).

Feel connection with the Seal, then say:

'In gratitude I come before You, Lord of the Universe. I know that You will grant this request for me through this holyTalisman of the great King Solomon. Amen'.

Attunement (First Time): 'In the Name of Father and Mother Divine, I receive the attunement to the 7th.Seal of Jupiter'. 'I ask the Creator to rectify my soul and purify it from impurities, harmful forces, and my fears. I am free from all difficulties and anxieties, I am protected and enveloped by divine protective light'.

Names of God for Attunement: Lamed.Alef.Vav (ל.א.ו), Cheit.Hei.Vav (ח.ה.ו), Nun.Lamed.Caf (נ.ל.ך), Alef.Nun.Yod (א.נ.י)

Activation (After First Time): 'In the Names of Father and Mother Divine, and of the Great King Solomon, I activate the 7th.Seal of Jupiter'.

1st. Seal of Venus: *Summons the right soulmate. Induces pure love and friendship between people, especially between couples, improves sexual vigour and summons the right soul mate to your life.*

'I invoke the angels: Nogahiel, to give me the ability to make friends, (or) to bring me my soul mate.

Acheliah, to enhance my personal magnetism so as to attract the attention of those I wish.

Socodiah, to give me the courage to be more interactive with my fellow man.

Nangariel, to keep my magical abilities high, so I can gain the love and admiration of others'.

Feel connection with the Seal, then say:

'Go you angels of this mighty seal go and fulfill my request and guide me in the name of the great King Solomon'.

Attunement (First Time): 'In the Name of Father and Mother Divine, I receive the attunement to the 1st.Seal of Venus'.
'Thanks to Creator I am surrounded of love and friends'.

Names of God for Attunement: Ayin.Lamed.Mem (ע.ל.מ), Mem.Hei.Shin (מ.ה.ש), Caf.Vav.Kof (כ.ו.ק), Samech.Yod.Teit (ס.י.ט)

Activation (After First Time): 'In the Names of Father and Mother Divine, and of the Great King Solomon, I activate the 1st.Seal of Venus'.

2nd. Seal of Venus: *Love among people and with God. Prompts love and compassion between people and between man and God. Brings its owner dignity, grace and fulfillment of wishes.*

'Put me as a sign upon your heart, as a sign of your arm, because love is as strong as death' (Songs of Songs 8:6)

Feel connection with the Seal, then say:

'I have grace and honour. Amen'.

Attunement (First Time): 'In the Name of Father and Mother Divine, I receive the attunement to the 2nd.Seal of Venus'. 'I invoke the Creator's power to achieve the desires of my heart'.

Names of God for Attunement: Alef.Caf.Alef (א.כ.א), Caf.Lamed.Yod (כ.ל.י), Lamed.Hei.Cheit (ל.ה.ח), Mem.Tzadi.Reish (מ.צ.ר)

Activation (After First Time): 'In the Names of Father and Mother Divine, and of the Great King Solomon, I activate the 2nd.Seal of Venus'.

3rd. Seal of Venus: *Fertility, fruitfulness at work. Helps to attract the love of a desirable person, brings love and admiration from those around you, good for all fertility issues, childbirth, fruitfulness at work and career.*

'And the Elohim blessed them, and the Elohim said unto them, 'Be ye fruitful, and multiply, and replenish the Earth and subdue it'. 'Oh Mighty YHVH-Adonai, the most powerful of names, I ask You to give me unlimited personal magnetism, more than I will ever need. Do so by the merit of the Great King Solomon'. 'Oh Mighty angels Ruach, Achides, Aegalmiel, Monachiel, and Dagaliel, I request you by the powers vested in this great seal of King Solomon, to bring me the love and admiration from those around me and make me fruitful at work'.

Feel connection with the Seal, then say:
'In gratitude I come before You YHVH, the Keeper of hearts. I know that You will grant this wish for me through this holy Talisman of the great King Solomon'.

Attunement (First Time): 'In the Name of Father and Mother Divine, I receive the attunement to the 3rd.Seal of Venus'. 'By the Creator's will I now attract my twin soul'.

Names of God for Attunement: Nun.Tav.Hei (נ.ת.ה), Lamed.Caf.Beit (ל.כ.ב), Samech.Alef.Lamed (ס.א. ל), Caf.Vav.Kof (כ.ו.ק)

Activation (After First Time): 'In the Names of Father and Mother Divine, and of the Great King Solomon, I activate the 3rd.Seal of Venus'.

4th. Seal of Venus: *Brings people together. Powerful for bringing people together from remote places and unifying them, helps difficulties in realizing marriage and solves marital problems in good spirits.*

'This is bone of my bones and flesh of my flesh, and they were one flesh' (Genesis 2:23,24).
'Oh Mighty YHVH - You who can soften and harden every person's heart. I ask You to send my loved one my way and have him/her irresistibly attracted to me. Do so by the merit of Your servant King Solomon'.

Feel connection with the Seal, then say:
'In gratitude, I come before You, YHVH, the Keeper of hearts. I know that You will grant this wish for me through this holy Talisman of Solomon Your servant'.

Attunement (First Time): 'In the Name of Father and Mother Divine, I receive the attunement to the 4th.Seal of Venus'. 'Divine wisdom now shines through me and I am full of love'.

Names of God for Attunement: Alef.Caf.Alef (א.כ.א), Mem.Beit.Hei (מ.ב. ה), Cheit.Beit.Vav (ח.ב.ו), Mem.Yod.Hei (מ.י. ה)

Activation (After First Time): 'In the Names of Father and Mother Divine, and of the Great King Solomon, I activate the 4th. Seal of Venus'.

5th. Seal of Venus: *Love, attraction and desire. Intensifies the desire of a loved one to you, makes your partner to fulfill your romantic wishes, and helps you become desirable by people.*

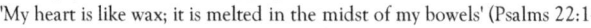

'My heart is like wax; it is melted in the midst of my bowels' (Psalms 22:14).

Feel connection with the Seal, then say:
'My beloved_____ will be attracted to me, by the power of this seal of the great King Solomon'.

Attunement (First Time): 'In the Name of Father and Mother Divine, I receive the attunement to the 5th.Seal of Venus '. 'I am now a pole of attraction for beauty and love'.

Names of God for Attunement: Lamed.Vav.Vav (ל.ו.ו), Mem.Lamed.Hei (מ.ל. ה), Ayin.Mem.Mem (ע.מ.ם), Hei.Reish.Yod (ה.ר.י)

Activation (After First Time): 'In the Names of Father and Mother Divine, and of the Great King Solomon, I activate the 5th.Seal of Venus '.

1st. Seal of Saturn: *Victory on negotiations. Defeats opponents at trial and negotiation and forces the rival to be responsive and obedient and fulfill your wishes.*

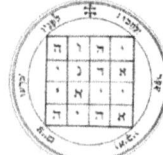

'May the desert tribes bow before Him, and His enemies lick the dust' (Psalms 72:9).

Feel connection with the Seal, then say:
'In gratitude I come before You Yahweh-Adonai. I know that You will grant this wish for me through this holy Talisman of Solomon Your servant'.

Attunement (First Time): 'In the Name of Father and Mother Divine, I receive the attunement to the 1st. Seal of Saturn'. 'I am grateful to the Creator for the persuasive power he gives me'.

Names of God for Attunement: Hei.Zain.Yod (ה.ז.י), Yod.Yod.Zayin (י.י.ז), Mem.Lamed.Hei (מ.ל. ה), Mem.Beit.Hei (מ.ב. ה)

Activation (After First Time): 'In the Names of Father and Mother Divine, and of the Great King Solomon, I activate the 1st.Seal of Saturn'.

2nd. Seal of Saturn: *Success in businesses. Gives power in any business engagement, enhances your persuasiveness and finding favour with rivals, helps you succeed in business and debates.*

'His dominion shall be from sea to sea, from the flood to the end of the world' (Psalm 72: 8).

Feel connection with the Seal, then say:
'In the Name of the Almighty God, grant this wish for me through this holy Talisman of Solomon Your servant'.

Attunement (First Time): 'In the Name of Father and Mother Divine, I receive the attunement to the 2nd.Seal of Saturn'. 'I invoke the Creator's power to increase my earnings and to receive subsistence'.

Names of God for Attunement: Samech.Alef.Lamed (ס.א.ל), Samech.Yod.Teit – (ס.י.ט), Mem.Lamed.Hei (מ.ל. ה), Mem.Cheit.Yod (מ.ח.י)

Activation (After First Time): 'In the Names of Father and Mother Divine, and of the Great King Solomon, I activate the 2nd.Seal of Saturn'.

3rd. Seal of Saturn: *Protection from witchcraft and psychic attacks. Protects against detractors who speak ill or you, conspiracies, curses, witchery, evil eye and any trouble imposed by other people.*

'I invoke the angels: <u>Omeliel</u> (who binds the spirits trying to harm me), <u>Anachiel</u> (protects me from people trying to harm me), <u>Arauchia</u> (protects from betrayals), and <u>Anatzachia</u> (protects me from all evils of others).

Feel connection with the Seal, then say:

'Go you angels <u>Omliel</u>, <u>Anachiel</u>, <u>Aruachia</u> and <u>Anatzachia</u> and protect me, and remember this holy seal of the great King Solomon'.

Attunement (First Time): 'In the Name of Father and Mother Divine, I receive the attunement to the 3rd. Seal of Saturn'. 'Evil entities that oppose me vanish and have no influence on me. I am guarded and protected by the Creator's will'.

Names of God for Attunement: Alef.Lamed.Dalet (א.ל.ד), Lamed.Alef.Vav (ל.א.ו), Reish.Yod.Yod (ר.י.י), Cheit.Ayin.Mem (ח.ע.ם).

Activation (After First Time): 'In the Names of Father and Mother Divine, and of the Great King Solomon, I activate the 3rd. Seal of Saturn'.

4th. Seal of Saturn: *Good decisions in your favour. Eliminates detracting forces, brings good news about decisions made in your favour, positive answers for interviews, exams and expectations.*

'Hear, Oh Israel: The LORD our God, the LORD is one (Deut.6:4).

'He wore cursing as his garment; it entered into his body like water, into his bones like oil (Psalms 109:18).

Feel connection with the Seal.

Attunement (First Time): 'In the Name of Father and Mother Divine, I receive the attunement to the 4th.Seal of Saturn'. 'I am filled with love and self-confidence and receive beautiful news'.

Names of God for Attunement: Hei.Reish.Yod (ה.ר.י), Mem.Yod.Hei (מ.י.ה), Samech.Alef.Lamed (ס.א.ל), Vav.Vav.Lamed (ו.ו.ל).

Activation (After First Time): 'In the Names of Father and Mother Divine, and of the Great King Solomon, I activate the 4th. Seal of Saturn'.

5th. Seal of Saturn: *Protects house, assets, body and soul. Guards the house and its contents from burglars, evil forces and damage, protect you precious assets against loss and harm to body and soul.*

'For the LORD, your God is God of gods and Lord of lords, the great God, and awesome, who shows no partiality and accepts no bribes (Deut.10:17).

'I invoke the angels: Arehanah, Rakhaniel, Roelhaiphar and Noaphiel'.

Feel connection with the Seal, then say:

'Go you angels of this mighty seal, go and protect me from all dangers that may come across my path, in the Name of Eloha-Yahweh. Amen'.

Attunement (First Time): 'In the Name of Father and Mother Divine, I receive the attunement to the 5th. Seal of Saturn'. 'The Creator protects my home and my temple'.

Names of God for Attunement: Lamed.Alef.Vav (ל.א.ו), Alef.Lamed.Dalet (א.ל.ד), Hei.Hei.Ayin (ה.ה.ע), Mem.Nun.Kof (מ.נ.ק).

Activation (After First Time): 'In the Names of Father and Mother Divine, and of the Great King Solomon, I activate the 5th. Seal of Saturn'.

6th. Seal of Saturn: *Keeps enemies away. This seal will inflict fear on a threatening person. Hold it in your right hand and say the enemy's name 7 times.*

'I have delivered him into the hands of the nations, he shall deal with him: I have cast him out according to his wickedness' (Ezekiel 31:11).

Feel connection with the Seal.

Attunement (First Time): 'In the Name of Father and Mother Divine, I receive the attunement to the 6th.Seal of Saturn'. 'Evil forces and negative presences disappear from my life. Nothing stands in my way or prevents me from achieving my goals'.

Names of God for Attunement: Yod.Lamed.Hei (י.ל.ה), Peh.Vav.Yod (פ.ו.י), Yod.Lamed.Yod (י.ל.י), Caf.Hei.Tav (כ.ה.ת).

Activation (After First Time): 'In the Names of Father and Mother Divine, and of the Great King Solomon, I activate the 6th. Seal of Saturn'.

7th. Seal of Saturn: *Stops Bad Luck. This seal will make your words to be heard in heaven. People will listen with respect and awe to what you say and trust your words.*

'Then the Earth trembled and shook, the bases of the hills also moved and were shaken, because He was angry' (Psalm 18:7). 'I invoke:

the Chayot Ha Kodesh (the Four Living Creatures), the Ophanim (the Wheels),
the Erelim (the Mighty Ones, the Thrones), the Chaschmalin (the Brilliant Ones, the Dominions),
the Seraphim (the Flaming Ones), the Melachim (the Virtues, the Kings),
the Elohim (the gods, the Principalities), the Beni Elohim (Sons of the Elohim), and
the Cherubim (the Archangels of Humanity).

Feel connection with the Seal.

Attunement (First Time): 'In the Name of Father and Mother Divine, I receive the attunement to the 7th. Seal of Saturn'. 'Thanks to the Creator I am now heard, in Heaven and on Earth'.

Names of God for Attunement: Mem.Lamed.Hei (מ.ל.ה), Yod.Reish.Tav (י.ר.ת), Nun.Nun.Alef (נ.נ.א), Mem.Beit.Hei (מ.ב.ה).

Activation (After First Time): 'In the Names of Father and Mother Divine, and of the Great King Solomon, I activate the 7th. Seal of Saturn'.

The Seals of King Solomon - One Page Chart

1st. Seal of The Sun	2nd. Seal of The Sun	3rd. Seal of The Sun	4th. Seal of The Sun	5th. Seal of The Sun	6th. Seal of The Sun	7th. Seal of The Sun
Magic & Control Over All Beings	Makes your Enemies Surrender to You	Fame, Fortune & Fulfillment of Wishes	Lets You See the Spirits at Work	Supernatural Transportability	Power of Invisibility	Release from Addiction

1st. Seal of the Moon	2nd. Seal of the Moon	3rd. Seal of the Moon	4th. Seal of the Moon	5th. Seal of the Moon	6th. Seal of the Moon
Opens Doors to Success, Cancels Spells	Protection from Natural Disasters	Protection from Poltergeists & Hauntings	Protects, Touches Crystals & Herbs	Protection During Sleep, Answers in Dreams	Brings Rain, Controls the Weather

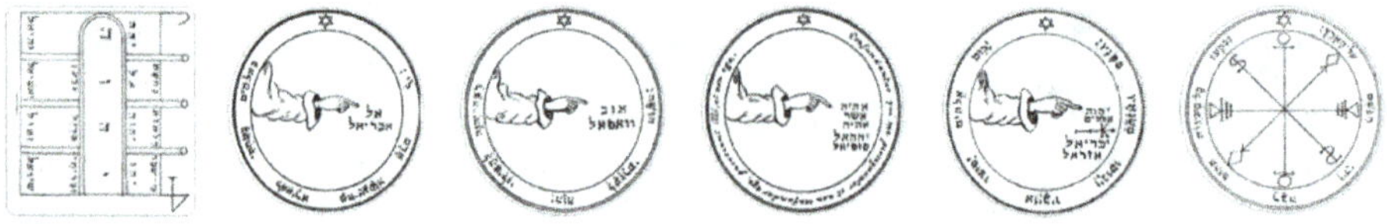

1st. Seal of Mars	2nd. Seal of Mars	3rd. Seal of Mars	4th. Seal of Mars	5th. Seal of Mars	6th. Seal of Mars	7th. Seal of Mars
Powers to Succeed in Chosen Path	Heals Diseases, Pain & Injuries	Success in Negotiations	Victory in Competitions	Magic Powers & Protection	Turns Opponents' Weapons Against Them	Confuses & Blinds Your Adversaries

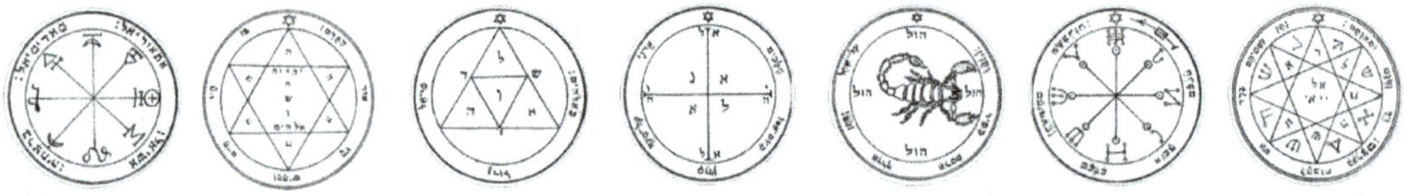

1st. Seal of Mercury	2nd. Seal of Mercury	3rd. Seal of Mercury	4th. Seal of Mercury	5th. Seal of Mercury
Personal Magnetism	Attain the Impossible	Influence with Words	Wisdom & Knowledge	Opens Doors & Portals (Spiritual & Physical)

1st. Seal of Jupiter	2nd. Seal of Jupiter	3rd. Seal of Jupiter	4th. Seal of Jupiter	5th. Seal of Jupiter	6th. Seal of Jupiter	7th. Seal of Jupiter
Success & Financial Abundance	Glory & Peace of Mind	Closes & Protects Houses	Great Financial Abundance	Spiritual & Psychic Powers	Protection from Earthly Dangers	Power Over Those Who Attempt to Fail You

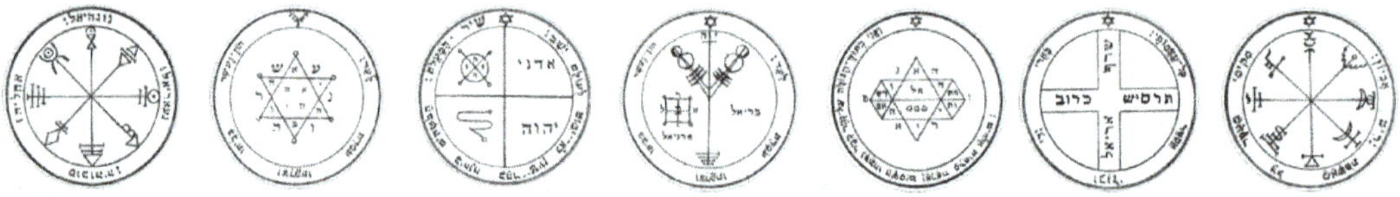

1st. Seal of Venus	2nd. Seal of Venus	3rd. Seal of Venus	4th. Seal of Venus	5th. Seal of Venus
Summons the Right Symbols	Love among People & with God	Fertility, Fruitfulness at Work	Brings People Together	Love, Attraction & Desire

1st. Seal of Saturn	2nd. Seal of Saturn	3rd. Seal of Saturn	4th. Seal of Saturn	5th. Seal of Saturn	6th. Seal of Saturn	7th. Seal of Saturn
Victory in Negotiations	Success in Business	Protection from Witchcraft & Psychic Attacks	Good Decisions in Your Favour	Protects Home, Assets, Body & Soul	Keeps Enemies Away	Stops Bad Luck

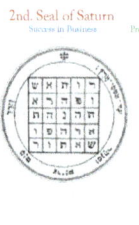

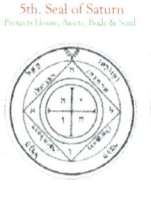

Part VI

Merkabah Mysticism

What is the Merkabah?

The Merkabah (also spelled Merkavah) refers to a type of mysticism rooted in Jewish esotericism, associated with the School of Early Jewish Mysticism. The word "Merkabah" means "chariot" in Hebrew and is thought to be a vehicle for spiritual ascension. It is derived from the visionary experiences described in the Book of Ezekiel, where the prophet describes his vision of a celestial chariot composed of heavenly beings and complex mechanical systems.

The word "Merkaba" is derived from the ancient Hebrew language, where "Mer" means light, "Ka" means spirit, and "Ba" means body. Together, the term represents the integration of spirit and body surrounded by light, indicating a vehicle or chariot. This concept is rooted in Judaic mysticism, particularly the Merkabah school of thought, which focuses on Ezekiel's vision from the Hebrew Bible. In this vision, the prophet Ezekiel describes a complex chariot composed of angels and interconnected wheels, moving through the heavens directed by the will of God.

The Merkaba is often depicted as two interlocked tetrahedrons, forming a three-dimensional Star of David. This geometric shape is significant in multiple spiritual traditions and is considered a vehicle for ascending or descending between spiritual realms. The intersecting tetrahedrons represent duality — masculine and feminine, earth and cosmos — merging together to create a dynamic field for spiritual transformation.

Historical Background

Merkabah mysticism originated in the first few centuries AD as a form of Jewish mysticism that focused on visions of the throne/chariot of God. It involves meditative techniques and rituals aimed at achieving heavenly ascents and acquiring esoteric knowledge from angelic beings.

In Kabbalistic practices, the Merkaba symbolizes the throne-chariot of God, the four-wheeled vehicle driven by four cherubim, each of which has four wings and four faces (of a man, lion, ox, and eagle). Kabbalists meditate on the Merkaba to ascend to higher realms and to gain deeper divine insights.

The Significance of Merkabah in Spiritual Practices

In modern esoteric teachings, the Merkaba is understood as a kind of "light spirit body," and activating it is believed to enable individuals to travel across different dimensions and protect the aura.

Merkabah mysticism is considered a means to connect with the divine, transcending the physical plane and accessing higher states of consciousness.

In the context of Kabbalah and Reiki, it can be seen as a profound tool for spiritual healing and transformation.

Techniques for Activating the Merkabah

1. **Meditation and Visualization:** Most practices involving the Merkaba begin with deep meditation, focusing on breathing and visualizing the energy field expanding from the body. Practitioners visualize the two tetrahedrons spinning in opposite directions to create a light field capable of carrying their consciousness to higher dimensions.

2. **Breathing Techniques:** Specific breathing patterns are used to activate the Merkaba. This often involves rhythmic breaths that increase energy flow and help to stabilize the rotating fields of the tetrahedrons.

3. **Intention and Emotional Clarity:** Setting clear intentions and maintaining a state of unconditional love and acceptance are crucial for effectively working with the Merkaba. The emotional state must align with higher spiritual frequencies to facilitate true ascension or spiritual experiences.

Applications of the Merkabah

Merkabah Mysticism, rooted in the deepest traditions of Jewish esotericism, holds an extraordinary potential for personal transformation and spiritual evolution. As the Merkabah (or 'Chariot') represents a complex, interdimensional spiritual vehicle, it provides practitioners with a profound tool for accessing higher dimensions of consciousness and engaging with the divine.

- **Spiritual Ascension:** The primary use of the Merkaba is for spiritual enlightenment and ascension, assisting practitioners in transcending physical laws to access higher spiritual levels.

The primary aim of Merkabah Mysticism in spiritual ascension is to elevate the soul to a state of higher spiritual awareness and closeness to the Divine. This journey begins with the activation of the Merkabah, envisioned as an interlocking grid of light and sacred geometry, surrounding and extending beyond the physical body. Through meditation, visualization, and the chanting of sacred mantras, practitioners can 'ride' this celestial chariot through the spiritual realms.

As one progresses in their Merkabah practices, the boundaries between the physical and spiritual worlds start to blur, offering glimpses into the interconnectedness of all life and the underlying spiritual fabric of the universe. This heightened awareness fosters a deep sense of unity and empathy, extending towards all beings, which is a hallmark of spiritual ascension.

☐ **Healing:** As a powerful energetic tool, the Merkaba is used for healing by aligning and balancing the chakras and the spiritual, mental, emotional, and physical bodies.

In the context of healing, Merkabah Mysticism serves as a powerful conduit for divine energy. By aligning the individual's energy fields with higher vibrational frequencies, the Merkabah facilitates profound healing transformations both at the physical and subtle energy levels. This alignment allows for the clearing of energy blockages, detoxification of negative energies, and the restoration of balance within the body's energetic system.

The geometric structure of the Merkabah is particularly conducive to healing because it acts as a resonant structure that amplifies healing intentions, much like a crystal grid. Practitioners can direct healing energies to specific areas of the body or emotional states, using the Merkabah to enhance the efficacy of other healing modalities, such as Reiki or crystal healing.

☐ **Protection:** The Merkaba field also serves as a protective shield around the practitioner, guarding against negative energies and enhancing spiritual growth.
The Merkabah is not only a vehicle for spiritual ascension but also a powerful protectorate. As a multidimensional light vehicle, the Merkabah field encases the practitioner in a sphere of divine energy, which acts as a formidable shield against external negative influences.

Energetic Shield: The Merkabah creates an energetic barrier that envelops the practitioner. This shield is composed of high-frequency vibrations that are inherently repulsive to lower, negative vibrations. By maintaining this high vibrational state, the Merkabah effectively prevents negative energies, psychic attacks, and emotional pollutants from penetrating the practitioner's spiritual and physical space.

Harmonization of Frequencies: The Merkabah also harmonizes the frequencies around the practitioner. This alignment mitigates the impact of external disharmonies, which often manifest as stress, conflict, or confusion. By creating a balanced energetic environment, the Merkabah helps the practitioner maintain mental clarity and emotional stability.

Activation for Protection: Regularly activating the Merkabah through meditation and visualization strengthens its capacity to shield. Practitioners can visualize the Merkabah spinning faster, which amplifies its protective properties. This can be particularly beneficial before entering into potentially harmful or energetically dense environments.

Intention Setting: Setting a clear intention for protection with the Merkabah is crucial. The practitioner should focus on the desired outcome of safety and security, instructing the Merkabah to act as a guardian against all that does not serve the highest good.

Use in Healing Spaces: For those involved in healing practices, the Merkabah can be used to cleanse and secure the healing space beforehand, ensuring that both practitioner and client are protected from any negative transference or leftover energies from previous sessions.

Enhanced Spiritual Growth: The protective nature of the Merkabah also contributes to spiritual growth by creating a safe energetic space for deep inner work. Without the interference of negative or disruptive energies, the practitioner can explore higher realms of consciousness more freely and deeply, fostering a stronger connection to the divine and accelerating their spiritual journey.

Creating a Sacred Space: By regularly using the Merkabah for protection, the practitioner sanctifies their immediate environment, turning it into a sacred space conducive to spiritual practices like prayer, meditation, and other rituals.

- **Integration of the Self:** Merkabah Mysticism encourages a holistic integration of the self, where spiritual insights and healing lead to a profound transformation of the individual's life and interactions with the world. As practitioners ascend spiritually and heal internally, they often report increased clarity, peace, and purpose in their daily lives.
This transformative journey also encourages a re-evaluation of personal values and life goals, aligning them more closely with one's spiritual purpose. As individuals become more attuned to their higher selves and the divine blueprint of their lives, they are better equipped to make decisions and engage in relationships that reflect their truest and most authentic selves.

In contemporary spiritual communities, the Merkaba is also integrated with other healing and meditative practices, including yoga, Reiki, and crystal healing, to enhance the effectiveness of these practices and promote overall well-being.

The transformative potential of Merkabah Mysticism is vast and deeply personal. It provides a path not only to spiritual enlightenment but also to profound healing and self-realization. By engaging with this ancient and sacred tradition, practitioners embark on a lifelong journey of learning, growth, and profound spiritual fulfillment.

Working with the Merkabah for Ascension

Step-by-Step Instructions

1. **Preparation and Purification:**
   - Begin with a period of ethical and spiritual self-assessment. This might involve fasting, prayer, and confession, as traditional Merkabah practices often require purity of body and mind.
   - Create a sacred space where you will not be disturbed, ensuring the environment is conducive to tranquility and spiritual work.

2. **Visualization and Meditation:**
   - Sit or lie in a comfortable position, close your eyes, and take deep breaths to reach a state of relaxation.
   - Visualize the Merkabah, often depicted as a star tetrahedron—a three-dimensional Star of David. Imagine it surrounding you, spinning slowly.
   - Focus on the Merkabah growing brighter and spinning faster as you visualize it ascending towards the spiritual realms.

3. **Chanting and Vibrational Alignment:**
   - Use sacred chants or mantras associated with Kabbalah or those you find personally powerful to align your vibrational energy with the Merkabah.
   - This chanting helps in focusing the mind and energizing the Merkabah vehicle.

4. **Spiritual Ascension:**
   - As you feel the Merkabah activate, imagine it taking you on a spiritual journey through different planes of existence. Each plane offers unique insights and divine wisdom.
   - Remain receptive to any messages or visions received during this journey.

5. **Integration and Grounding:**
   - After completing your ascension journey, visualize the Merkabah slowly descending back to your physical environment.
   - Take several deep breaths to ground yourself, and gradually open your eyes.
   - Record any insights or experiences in your spiritual diary.

Healing with the Merkabah

Merkabah Mysticism is not only a pathway to spiritual ascension but also a powerful framework for healing. The Merkabah, with its geometric precision and divine origins, serves as a potent tool for channeling healing energy across multiple dimensions of human existence—physical, emotional, mental, and spiritual.

In a nutshell, this is how we can work with the Merkabah:

- Envision the Merkabah surrounding the person or yourself needing healing.
- Channel Reiki energy or divine light through the Merkabah, directing it towards healing physical, emotional, or spiritual issues.
- The geometric structure of the Merkabah can be visualized as amplifying and directing this healing energy efficiently.

We will now delve deeper into the specific techniques for engaging with the Merkabah:

Physical Healing

When applied to physical healing, the Merkabah can be visualized surrounding the body or specific parts of the body that require healing. The geometric shape of the Merkabah, especially its dual tetrahedrons spinning in opposite directions, helps in creating a vortex of energy that can cleanse and rejuvenate the physical cells, tissues, and organs.

- **Technique:** Envision the Merkabah spinning rapidly to generate a healing light that penetrates the affected areas, dissolving any blockages or diseased energies, and restoring the natural flow of life force (prana or chi) throughout the body.

Emotional and Mental Healing

Emotional and mental healing is crucial in our journey towards wholeness. The Merkabah facilitates this by helping to balance and harmonize the emotional body and mental states. It works by aligning the heart and mind, which is essential for overcoming emotional distress and achieving mental clarity.

- **Technique:** Visualize the Merkabah enveloping your emotional or mental space in a soothing light, gently lifting away fears, anxieties, and negative thoughts. As it spins, imagine the Merkabah infusing this space with positive energy and peace, stabilizing emotions and fostering a sense of profound inner calm.

Spiritual Healing

At the spiritual level, the Merkabah can open gateways to higher consciousness, facilitating deep insights and connections with the divine. This aspect of healing often involves clearing spiritual blockages and enhancing one's spiritual gifts.

- **Technique:** During meditation, focus on the Merkabah ascending through various spiritual planes, each represented by different colors and vibrations. Allow the Merkabah to guide your consciousness to these realms, where healing can occur directly from spiritual beings or through profound self-realizations.

Healing Through Dimensional Access

One of the unique aspects of healing with the Merkabah is its ability to access different dimensions and timelines. This can be particularly powerful for addressing karmic and ancestral issues that may be impacting an individual's health and well-being.

- **Technique:** Use guided meditations to travel within the Merkabah to specific times or places where traumas were originated or where healing needs to be applied. Through this journey, seek to understand, reconcile, and heal these past influences, bringing back wisdom and healing energy to the present.

Integration and Grounding

After any healing session using the Merkabah, it's important to ensure that the energies are properly integrated and that one is fully grounded. This helps in realizing the full benefits of the healing energies and maintaining the equilibrium between one's energetic and physical presence.

- **Technique:** Conclude each session by visualizing the Merkabah gently descending back to the earthly plane, bringing with it the healing energies and insights from higher realms. Imagine these energies being absorbed into the body, mind, and spirit. Finally, engage in grounding activities, such as walking barefoot on the earth or consuming grounding foods.

Advanced Visualization Techniques

As we explore the sacred Merkabah, I encourage you to deepen your geometric visualizations. Consider the dual tetrahedrons of the Merkabah, interlocking with one pointing upwards to the heavens and the other grounding downwards to Earth. This balance between the physical and spiritual realms is crucial for your ascension practices.

Incorporating colour into your visualizations can also amplify your intentions. Envisioning the Merkabah in violet can tap into higher spiritual energies, while green may facilitate healing.

Detailed Visualization of the Merkabah's Structure

To enhance your meditative and healing work with the Merkabah, engage in detailed visualization of its structure. Imagine each edge, vertex, and face of the tetrahedrons with crystal clarity. See them as composed of light, perhaps shimmering with energy or pulsating with life. Visualize these geometric forms not as static, but as dynamic, living symbols that breathe and move with your breath.

Dynamic Movement in Visualization

- Spinning Tetrahedrons: Picture the two tetrahedrons of the Merkabah spinning in opposite directions. The upward-pointing tetrahedron spins clockwise, while the downward-pointing one spins counterclockwise. This rotation generates a powerful energy vortex that can elevate your consciousness to higher dimensions.
- Expansion and Contraction: During your visualization, see the Merkabah expanding to encompass a larger energetic field, then contracting to intensify the energy within. This pulsation helps synchronize your energy field with that of the universal flow, enhancing your ability to manifest and heal.

Incorporating Multiple Colors for Specific Intentions

- Blue for Communication: Visualize a blue light within the Merkabah when working on throat chakra issues, enhancing communication and self-expression.
- Red for Vitality: Introduce a red glow to stimulate physical energy, grounding, and vitality, particularly useful for root chakra activation.
- Gold for Divine Connection: A golden light can be visualized to connect more deeply with divine wisdom and cosmic intelligence, aligning with the crown chakra.

Visualization of Merkabah's Journey Through the Chakras

For a profound alignment of your energy centers, visualize the Merkabah moving through each chakra, starting from the base and rising up to the crown. As it moves through each chakra, imagine it spinning and clearing any blockages, aligning the chakras and infusing them with vibrant energy.

Use of Affirmations with Visualization

Combine your visualizations with spoken or mentally recited affirmations to strengthen the intentions behind them. For example, as you visualize the Merkabah in violet, affirm, "I am open to receiving spiritual wisdom and guidance." For green, you might use, "I am healing deeply and completely."

Incorporating Sacred Geometry

Understanding the principles of sacred geometry associated with the Merkabah, such as the significance of the Flower of Life, enriches our connection to this mystical symbol. Applying these principles in other spiritual and healing contexts can enhance the holistic nature of our practices.

Deeper Insights into the Flower of Life

The Flower of Life, a geometrical figure composed of multiple evenly-spaced, overlapping circles arranged in a flower-like pattern, is considered one of the most profound geometrical images of ancient and modern times. It is visually representative of the connections life weaves through all sentient beings, believed by some to contain ancient, religious value depicting the fundamental forms of space and time.

- **Integration with the Merkabah:** Visualize the Merkabah as emerging from the Flower of Life. This connection highlights the belief that all life and consciousness arise from a single source, mirrored in the interlocking tetrahedrons of the Merkabah which point to the unity of spirit and matter.

Geometric Patterns in Healing Spaces

Sacred geometry can be applied to create and enhance healing spaces. Using symbols like the Flower of Life on the floors or walls can serve to amplify the energies within the space, making it conducive to deeper spiritual work and healing.

- **Energetic Grids:** Create energetic grids by placing crystals at points along the patterns of sacred geometry, which can be activated during healing sessions to intensify the healing energies and assist in aligning the chakras.

Practical Applications in Meditation

Incorporating sacred geometry in meditation involves visualizing geometrical patterns that align with the body's energy fields, enhancing meditation depth and effectiveness.

- **Meditative Focus:** Use the visual of the Flower of Life to center your meditative focus. This can help in harmonizing your personal energy field with the cosmic grid, promoting spiritual awakening and insight.

Sacred Geometry in Art and Decor

Including sacred geometry in your environment through art or decor can subtly shift the energy of your space. These symbols act not only as beautiful artistic expressions but also as functional tools that enhance the spiritual and healing quality of the environment.

- **Environmental Harmony:** Placing symbols like the Merkabah or the Flower of Life in areas where you practice meditation or healing work can help to maintain a high vibrational, sacred space.

Educational Use

Teaching the concepts of sacred geometry can help others see their own lives and experiences reflected in these universal patterns, fostering a deeper understanding of the interconnectedness of all things.

- **Workshops and Classes:** Offer workshops that explore sacred geometry's role in personal and spiritual development, using the Merkabah and Flower of Life as core examples of how these patterns manifest in both theoretical and practical applications.

Connection with Angelic Realms

In our meditations, we can reach out to the angelic realms for guidance and protection. Specifically, connecting with Archangel Metatron, who is closely associated with the Merkabah, deepens our spiritual journey and provides profound insights.

Understanding Archangel Metatron

Archangel Metatron is known as the angel of life and the scribe of God, overseeing the flow of energy in a mystical light cube known as "Metatron's Cube," which contains all of the geometric shapes in God's creation and represents the patterns that make up everything God has made. This cube is closely associated with the Merkabah due to its sacred geometric forms.

- **Role in Ascension:** Metatron guides those who are navigating the spiritual process known as ascension, helping them to harmonize their physical existence with their higher spiritual purposes.

- **Connection Through the Merkabah:** When meditating on the Merkabah, invoking Metatron can enhance the clarity and reach of your spiritual inquiries, offering protection and wisdom.

Techniques for Connecting with Metatron

- **Visualization:** Visualize a brilliant white light descending from above, symbolizing Metatron's presence. As you focus on the Merkabah, imagine it radiating this divine light, strengthening your connection to Metatron.

- **Chanting and Prayer:** Use specific chants or prayers dedicated to Metatron to invite his guidance and protection. Chanting his name in your meditations can amplify your intentions and create a vibrational match for his energy.

Engaging Other Angelic Beings

While Metatron is a key figure in working with the Merkabah, other angels can also be invoked for their specific energies and assistance:

- **Archangel Raphael:** Call upon Raphael for healing physical, emotional, or spiritual ailments during your Merkabah meditation.

- **Archangel Michael:** Seek Michael's protection against any negative or lower energies you wish to guard against during spiritual work.

- **Archangel Gabriel:** Engage Gabriel for clarity and purity of purpose, especially when seeking insights during Merkabah activations.

Group Meditation for Enhanced Connection

- **Collective Intentions:** Organize group meditations that focus on connecting with the angelic realms through the Merkabah. The collective energy of a group can significantly amplify the connection, making the experience more profound.

- **Guided Angelic Meditations:** Offer guided sessions where participants are led through a series of visualizations and invocations that foster a deeper connection with Metatron and other angels.

Integrating Angelic Insights

After reaching out to these celestial beings, it is crucial to integrate the insights and guidance received:

- **Journaling:** Encourage practitioners to journal their experiences and any messages received from the angelic realms immediately after meditation. This helps in grounding the insights and translating them into actionable guidance.

- **Sharing Experiences:** Create a forum or a discussion group where individuals can share their experiences and insights gained from angelic connections. This not only validates their experiences but also helps in collective learning and spiritual growth.

Breathing Exercises and Mantras

Here we have some specific breathing techniques that synchronize with the Merkabah's rotational movements, enhancing the flow of energy and deepening our meditation practice. Using mantras, especially ancient Hebrew prayers, can protect and empower us during our spiritual journeys.

Detailed Breathing Techniques

Breathing exercises are foundational in harnessing the energy of the Merkabah. By synchronizing your breath with the movements of the Merkabah, you can enhance your energetic intake and stabilization.

- **Rotational Breathing:** Visualize the Merkabah spinning around you. As you inhale, imagine drawing in cosmic energy through the top tetrahedron, letting it spiral down to your heart. As you exhale, envision this energy radiating out through the bottom tetrahedron, anchoring you to the Earth.

- **Rhythmic Breathing:** Establish a rhythmic breathing pattern that mirrors the pulsating energy of the Merkabah. This could be in counts of four for inhaling, holding, and exhaling, which helps maintain a steady flow of energy and prepares the mind for deeper meditative states.

Utilizing Mantras

Mantras are powerful tools for protection, healing, and spiritual elevation. By reciting specific sacred texts or phrases, you can align more closely with divine energies.

- **Hebrew Mantras:** Incorporate ancient Hebrew prayers that resonate with the Merkabah's energy. For example, the Shema Yisrael ("Hear, O Israel") prayer can be used to invoke unity and protection during meditation.

- **Personalized Mantras:** Create personalized mantras that reflect your spiritual intentions or desired outcomes. These could be simple affirmations like "I am aligned with my highest good" or more elaborate prayers that invoke specific angels or spiritual guides.

Integration of Mantras with Breathing

Combining mantras with breathing exercises creates a powerful synergy that can significantly enhance your spiritual practice.

- **Mantra during Inhale/Exhale:** Choose a mantra to recite mentally while inhaling, and another for exhaling. This dual-focus helps to deepen concentration and reinforces the mantra's energy within your body and spirit.

- **Chanting Out Loud:** For some practices, chanting out loud while engaging in deep breathing exercises can help to clear the space of negative energies and fill it with your intention.

Protective and Empowering Aspects

Mantras not only enhance meditation but also offer protection and empowerment.

- **Protective Circle:** While performing your breathing exercises, visualize a circle of light formed by the recitation of mantras around you, creating a protective barrier against any negative or intrusive energies.

- **Empowerment through Repetition:** Regular repetition of these mantras during breathing exercises can strengthen your spiritual presence, grounding you in your practice and empowering your spiritual path.

Integration with Other Spiritual Practices

Combining the Merkabah with Reiki practices allows us to channel enhanced healing and spiritual ascension energies. I also encourage you to blend Merkabah meditations with other modalities you are familiar with, such as crystal healing or tarot, to create a more comprehensive spiritual practice.

Combining Merkabah and Reiki

Reiki, a well-known healing technique that channels universal life energy, can be greatly enhanced through the integration with Merkabah meditation. This combination allows for a deeper energy flow and can help in aligning the chakras more effectively.

- **Technique:** During a Reiki session, visualize the Merkabah surrounding the recipient. This visualization can help focus and intensify the healing energy, directing it more precisely to areas that require healing.

Merkabah and Crystal Healing

Crystals are powerful tools that resonate with specific frequencies and can amplify the Merkabah's energy.

- **Crystals as Amplifiers:** Use crystals like clear quartz, which can hold and amplify the intention of your Merkabah meditation. Arrange these crystals around your meditation space or hold them while meditating to enhance the connection.
- **Energy Grids:** Create crystal grids in the shape of the Merkabah to amplify and direct energies during both meditation and healing sessions.

Integrating Tarot for Insight and Guidance

Tarot cards can provide deep insights and guidance for your spiritual practices with the Merkabah.

- **Guidance for Meditation:** Before beginning a Merkabah meditation, draw a tarot card to receive guidance on what to focus on or understand during your meditation.
- **Reflective Practice:** Use the insights from tarot readings post-meditation to reflect on your spiritual journey and how it aligns with the messages or themes from the reading.

Merkabah in Astrology and Numerology

Incorporating astrological or numerological aspects can provide personalized insights into how to best work with the Merkabah based on one's astrological signs or life path numbers.

- **Astrological Alignments:** Consider the positions of planets and their energies when planning Merkabah meditations to harness specific cosmic energies.
- **Numerological Harmonies:** Use numerology to determine the most auspicious times or days for Merkabah meditations, enhancing the efficacy of your spiritual practices.

Creating a Holistic Spiritual Routine

Combining these diverse practices allows for a more holistic approach to spirituality, where the strengths of one practice can support and enhance the others.

- **Routine Development:** Develop a daily or weekly routine that incorporates various elements of these practices, adjusting as needed based on your spiritual needs and the insights gained from ongoing practice.
- **Workshops and Sharing Sessions:** Facilitate workshops or sharing sessions where participants can learn about integrating these modalities and share their experiences and outcomes, fostering a community of learning and spiritual growth.

Ethical Considerations and Safety

It is essential to approach Merkabah practices with humility and respect, recognizing the profound nature of this tool. Always ensure to ground yourself after meditations, reconnecting with your physical state and earthly energies to remain balanced and centred.

Ethical Engagement with the Merkabah

- **Respect for the Sacred:** Recognize the Merkabah as a sacred geometric structure that is not merely a tool but a spiritual entity in itself. Approach each session with reverence, understanding that you are engaging with a powerful spiritual symbol that transcends ordinary reality.

- **Intention Setting:** Before engaging in any Merkabah practice, set clear and positive intentions. This helps ensure that the energies invoked and practices undertaken are for the highest good of all involved, avoiding any misuse of the profound energies at play.

Safety Protocols

- **Physical Preparedness:** Ensure that you are physically well and in a safe environment before beginning any Merkabah practices. This includes being well-rested, hydrated, and in a space where you will not be disturbed.

- **Psychological Readiness:** Given the powerful nature of Merkabah meditations, ensure you are mentally and emotionally prepared. This might involve doing lighter meditation or relaxation exercises if you feel overwhelmed or stressed.

Grounding Techniques

- **Physical Grounding:** After a Merkabah session, engage in physical activities that help reconnect with the earthly energies. This can include walking barefoot on the ground, gardening, or even gentle stretching.

- **Nutritional Grounding:** Consuming grounding foods after meditative practices, such as root vegetables or herbal teas, can also help restore balance between your energetic and physical bodies.

Responsibility Towards Others

- **Sharing Knowledge with Integrity:** When teaching Merkabah practices, ensure that your students are aware of the ethical considerations and are sufficiently prepared to handle the energies involved.

- **Monitoring Energy Impact:** Be observant of the impact that Merkabah practices have on yourself and others. If negative effects are observed, reassess the approach and consider integrating more grounding or cleansing practices.

Legal and Cultural Sensitivity

- **Cultural Appropriation:** Be mindful of the origins of the Merkabah within Jewish mysticism. When incorporating it into practices derived from or inspired by other cultural backgrounds, do so with sensitivity and respect towards its historical and cultural significance.

- **Legal Compliance:** Ensure that any public gathering or workshop involving Merkabah practices complies with local regulations, especially if it involves large groups or public spaces.

Part VII

Gematria

What is Gematria?

Unlocking Spiritual Insights Through Numbers

Gematria is a mystical numerological system used within Kabbalah that assigns numerical value to words, phrases, or letters. This practice allows us to explore deeper spiritual meanings and connections by calculating these values. Gematria can reveal hidden messages and insights within Hebrew texts, which are believed to be the language of creation.

Principles of Gematria

- **Numerical Correspondence**: Each letter in the Hebrew alphabet is associated with a specific number. When letters of words are added together, they form a numerical value that can be interpreted spiritually.

- **Vibrational Harmony**: Just as Reiki believes in the healing power of energy vibrations, Gematria emphasizes the vibrational essence of numbers. These vibrations can influence and enhance spiritual and physical well-being.

Applying Gematria in Kabbalah Reiki

- **Healing with Numbers**: Practitioners can use the numerical values of a client's name or significant life dates to tailor healing sessions. Understanding these numbers helps align the healing energies more precisely with the client's spiritual needs.

- **Creating Personal Mantras**: By calculating the Gematria of key spiritual words or phrases, practitioners can create powerful mantras for meditation and healing. These mantras can be used to focus energy, invoke protection, and facilitate deeper spiritual connections.

Gematria in Practice: Step-by-Step

1. **Choosing a Word or Phrase**: Start with a Hebrew word or phrase related to the healing intent or spiritual question at hand.

2. **Calculating Numerical Value**: Assign each letter its corresponding numerical value and sum them up.

3. **Interpreting the Meaning**: Use traditional interpretations of these numbers to derive spiritual insights or guidance. This might involve consulting classical Kabbalistic texts or reliable Gematria sources.

Case Studies

Case Study 1: Healing with a Personal Name

Background: Sarah, a client experiencing chronic stress and anxiety, sought a deeper spiritual approach to her healing. Her Hebrew name, שרה (Sarah), was chosen for the Gematria analysis to uncover deeper spiritual dimensions of her challenges.

Process:

1. **Gematria Calculation**: The Hebrew letters of Sarah (שרה) are Shin (300=ש), Reish (200=ר), and He (5=ה). Adding these together, the Gematria of Sarah is 505.

2. **Interpretation**: In Kabbalistic terms, the number 505 resonates with themes of transformation and healing. It shares the same numerical value as the word "אורח" (Orach, meaning "path" in Hebrew), suggesting a journey or progression.

3. **Reiki Session**: During the Reiki sessions, specific focus was placed on the path of healing, envisioning the energy clearing blockages along Sarah's spiritual path. Mantras associated with progression and journey were used to enhance the session's intent.

Outcome: Sarah reported a significant reduction in anxiety levels and a newfound clarity in her life's direction. She felt more aligned with her spiritual path and reported experiencing a sense of unfolding and transformation following the sessions.

Case Study 2: Focusing on a Significant Date

Background: Mark, dealing with significant life decisions around his career, chose to explore the significance of his upcoming birthday—March 3rd (03/03)—using Gematria to gain insights and guidance.

Process:

1. **Date Numerology**: The date 03/03 translates numerologically to 303.

2. **Gematria Calculation**: In Hebrew, the number 303 corresponds to the word "אמת" (Emet, meaning "truth").

3. **Reiki Session**: The Reiki treatment was designed around the theme of "truth", helping Mark to align with his true desires and career aspirations. Reiki symbols for clarity and decision-making were integrated throughout the session.

Outcome: Mark felt a powerful alignment during and after the session. He reported feeling more confident and clear about his career path, stating that the session helped him connect with his inner truth and guided him toward making decisions that felt right on a profound level.

Part VIII

Ethical Practice and Professional Development

Ethical Guidelines for Kabbalah Reiki

Ethical Considerations

Practicing Kabbalah Reiki requires a strong ethical foundation to ensure that both practitioners and clients experience the most beneficial and respectful interactions. Adhering to these ethical guidelines is crucial for fostering trust, respect, and professionalism in your practice.

Principle of Do No Harm

- **Safety First**: Always prioritize the well-being of the client. This includes physical, emotional, and spiritual safety. Avoid any practices or actions that could potentially harm the client.

- **Informed Consent**: Ensure that all clients provide informed consent before beginning treatment. Clearly explain what Kabbalah Reiki involves, what they should expect during a session, and any potential risks.

Confidentiality and Privacy

- **Safeguarding Information**: Maintain the confidentiality of all client information. This includes personal details, session notes, and any sensitive information disclosed during therapy.

- **Privacy in Practice**: Use secure methods to store and handle client information. Be transparent with clients about how their information is used and stored.

Respect for Autonomy

- **Client-Centered Practice**: Empower clients to make their own decisions regarding their health and spiritual practices. Provide all necessary information to help them make informed choices without imposing your own beliefs.

- **Respect Boundaries**: Be attentive to and respectful of the client's boundaries, and adjust practices accordingly. This includes recognizing and honoring their comfort levels during physical touch and energy work.

Professionalism, Integrity and Self-Care

- **Ongoing Learning:** Commit to ongoing professional development to deepen your understanding of Kabbalah Reiki and related fields. This enhances your effectiveness and the quality of care provided.

- **Honest Representation:** Accurately represent your skills, qualifications, and the potential benefits of Kabbalah Reiki without exaggerating or providing guarantees about the outcomes.

- **Practitioner Wellbeing:** Engage in regular self-care practices. A well-balanced practitioner is better equipped to assist others and maintain a high standard of practice.

Cultural Sensitivity

- **Cultural Competence:** Develop an understanding and respect for the cultural backgrounds of your clients. Recognize and honor the diverse beliefs and practices clients may bring to a session.

- **Inclusive Practices:** Make your practice welcoming and accessible to individuals from all backgrounds. Avoid cultural appropriation by respecting the origins and contexts of practices and symbols used within Kabbalah Reiki.

Accountability

- **Self-Reflection:** Regularly reflect on your practice to continually improve and adhere to these ethical standards.

- **Peer Consultation:** Engage with peers for consultation and feedback, especially when faced with ethical dilemmas or challenging situations.

Handling Ethical Dilemmas

- **Ethical Decision-Making Framework:** Establish a clear process for making ethical decisions. This may include consulting with experienced practitioners, referring to ethical guidelines, and considering the potential impacts of decisions on all involved.

- **Reporting and Resolving Issues:** Have a system in place for addressing and resolving any complaints or ethical issues that arise. Ensure transparency in how these issues are handled to maintain trust and accountability.

Setting Boundaries with Clients

Setting appropriate boundaries with clients is essential for maintaining a professional and ethical practice in any therapeutic or healing setting, including Kabbalah Reiki. These boundaries help protect both the practitioner and the client, ensuring that the relationship remains focused on healing and growth.

Importance of Professional Boundaries

- **Defining the Relationship:** Clearly define the professional nature of the relationship from the outset. This helps to manage expectations and prevents misunderstandings related to the roles of both the practitioner and the client.

- **Consistency in Conduct:** Apply professional boundaries consistently with all clients. This consistency helps in creating a safe and trustworthy environment.

Types of Boundaries

- **Emotional Boundaries:** Avoid becoming emotionally involved with your clients beyond the empathetic connection required to facilitate healing. Maintain an objective stance while remaining compassionate and supportive.
- **Physical Boundaries:** Be explicit about the use of touch, explaining its purpose in Kabbalah Reiki and ensuring it is always appropriate and consensual. Physical boundaries are particularly crucial to respect personal space and comfort.
- **Social Boundaries:** Keep your relationship with clients professional. This means not engaging in social relationships outside of the therapeutic context, which could compromise the integrity of the healing process.
- **Financial Boundaries:** Establish clear agreements regarding fees, payment methods, and session schedules before starting treatment. Avoid any financial dealings that could create conflicts of interest or misunderstandings.

Communicating Boundaries

- **Clear Communication:** Discuss these boundaries during the initial consultation and reinforce them as needed throughout the therapeutic relationship. Clear communication helps prevent boundary crossings that might occur unintentionally.
- **Documentation:** It's useful to have written guidelines regarding boundaries as part of your intake forms or welcome packets. This ensures that clients are aware of your policies from the beginning.

Handling Boundary Crossings

- **Recognition and Action:** If a boundary has been crossed, recognize it immediately and take steps to address the situation. Discuss the issue with the client directly and clearly, reinforcing the boundaries respectfully but firmly.
- **Consultation and Supervision:** In cases of uncertainty about how to handle potential boundary issues, seek advice from experienced colleagues, supervisors, or mentors within your professional community.

Self-Reflection

- **Regular Reviews:** Regularly reflect on your interactions with clients to ensure that you are maintaining appropriate boundaries. Self-reflection helps identify any areas where boundaries may be becoming blurred and allows for corrective action.

Training and Education

- **Boundary Education:** Engage in ongoing education and training on professional boundaries. Workshops and courses on ethics in therapeutic practices can provide valuable insights and strategies for setting and maintaining boundaries.

Part IX

Meditation, Lifestyle, and Continued Learning

Meditation and Visualization Guided Practices for Kabbalah Reiki

Introduction to Meditation and Visualization

Meditation and visualization are fundamental practices in Kabbalah Reiki, serving as powerful tools to enhance spiritual awareness and facilitate deep healing. These practices help practitioners and clients align their energy, focus their intentions, and connect more deeply with the spiritual dimensions.

The Role of Meditation in Kabbalah Reiki

- **Centering and Grounding**: Meditation helps practitioners and clients center themselves and establish a grounded state, essential for effective energy work.

- **Enhancing Intuitive Abilities**: Regular meditation practice sharpens intuition, a key aspect of guiding Reiki healing and interpreting spiritual insights.

The Power of Visualization

- **Creating Healing Imagery**: Visualization involves forming mental images that promote healing and energetic balance. It can be used to envision healing energy surrounding and penetrating the body or to picture the balancing of chakras.

- **Symbolic Visualization**: In Kabbalah Reiki, practitioners often use symbols from Kabbalistic mysticism within their visualizations to enhance the spiritual power of their sessions.

Guided Meditations and Visualizations

Preparing for Guided Practices

- **Setting the Space**: Ensure the space is quiet, comfortable, and free from interruptions. You might use candles, incense, or soft background music to enhance the ambiance.

- **Physical Readiness**: Encourage participants to sit or lie in a comfortable position and close their eyes. Deep, calming breaths help in relaxing the body before starting the visualization.

Example Guided Meditation: Healing Light Visualization

1. **Introduction**: Begin by guiding participants to breathe deeply, inhaling peace and exhaling tension.

2. **Body Scan**: Slowly guide awareness through each part of the body, encouraging relaxation and a sense of ease.

3. **Envisioning the Healing Light**:
    - Instruct participants to visualize a gentle, glowing light above their heads.
    - Visualize this light descending slowly, enveloping the body in warmth and healing energy.
    - Imagine the light specifically targeting areas of pain or imbalance, restoring and rejuvenating every cell.

4. **Expansion of Light**: Gradually expand this light beyond the physical body, imagining it forming a protective aura that shields against negative energy.

5. **Closing**: Slowly bring awareness back to the present, focusing on the breath and physical sensations, before gently opening the eyes.

Example Guided Visualization: Chakra Balancing

1. **Starting the Visualization**: Begin with deep breathing to center and ground the participant.

2. **Visualizing Each Chakra**:
    - Start at the root chakra, envisioning a vibrant red light spinning and growing in intensity.
    - Move sequentially up to the crown chakra, using associated colors and visualizing each chakra in turn, spinning in harmony and perfectly aligned.

3. **Energy Alignment**: Visualize a beam of light connecting all chakras, harmonizing personal energy with universal energy.

4. **Conclusion**: The aim here is to obtain a sense of completeness and alignment, then gently return to the room feeling balanced and energized.

Tips for Effective Guided Sessions

- **Use Descriptive Language**: Rich, descriptive language helps participants vividly imagine scenes and enhances the effectiveness of the visualization.

- **Be Flexible**: Adapt the guidance based on the feedback and energy you perceive from the participants whenever you are guiding the sessions.

- **Practice Regularly**: I would encourage regular practice to deepen the effectiveness and personal connection to the visualizations.

Dietary and Lifestyle Recommendations

Balancing the body's energy through Kabbalah Reiki is not only about spiritual practices but also about nurturing the physical vessel which holds our spirit. A balanced diet and healthy lifestyle can significantly enhance the effectiveness of Reiki by maintaining the body's natural equilibrium and vitality.

Nutritional Guidance

- **Whole Foods**: I would encourage a diet rich in whole foods. This includes fruits, vegetables, whole grains, nuts, seeds, and legumes, which provide essential nutrients and energy without the heavy energetic burden that processed foods often carry.
- **Hydration**: Staying hydrated is crucial for maintaining the flow of energy through the body. I would recommend drinking plenty of water throughout the day to support the body's natural detox processes and improve energy flow.
- **Mindful Eating**: I would encourage eating with mindfulness and gratitude. Being present during meals and appreciating the food's journey from earth to table can enhance its nourishing qualities and support spiritual practices.

Lifestyle Adjustments

- **Regular Exercise**: Regular physical activity helps to keep the energy channels within the body clear and active. Gentle, meditative forms of exercise like yoga, Tai Chi, or walking in nature can be particularly beneficial for maintaining balance and grounding.
- **Adequate Rest**: I would like to emphasize the importance of getting enough rest. Sleep is a fundamental healing process for the mind, body, and spirit, allowing for rejuvenation and natural energy alignment.
- **Stress Management**: Since stress can significantly block or deplete a person's energy, incorporating regular stress-reduction techniques such as meditation, deep breathing exercises, or journaling is recommended.

Avoiding Toxins

- **Limit Intake of Toxins**: I would recommend on reducing the intake of substances that can cloud or deplete energy, such as excessive caffeine, alcohol, tobacco, and processed sugars.
- **Natural Products**: I would suggest the use of natural, non-toxic products for personal care and home cleaning to reduce the exposure to synthetic chemicals that can affect both physical and energetic health.

Spiritual Hygiene

- **Regular Cleansing Practices**: Just as one cleanses their physical body, I woud recommend regular energetic cleansings through practices such as smudging with sage, taking salt baths, or using crystals like selenite and black tourmaline to clear negative energies.
- **Environment**: I would also encourage creating a peaceful and organized living and working environment, which can enhance the flow of positive energy and reduce stress.

Community and Relationships

- **Supportive Relationships**: I would advise you on cultivating relationships that are supportive and nurturing. I would encourage spending time with those who uplift and inspire, as this can greatly enhance personal energy and well-being.
- **Community Involvement**: I would suggest engaging in community service or group activities that align with your spiritual values. Being part of a community can provide a sense of belonging and purpose, vital for mental and spiritual health.

Continued Learning and Development

Continued learning and development are vital for anyone involved in Kabbalah Reiki, whether you are a beginner or an experienced practitioner. The journey of healing and spiritual growth is ongoing, and deepening your knowledge and skills can greatly enhance your practice and the support you offer to others.

Lifelong Learning Philosophy

- **Commitment to Growth**: It is important to view learning as a lifelong journey. Practitioners should remain students of life and spirituality, continually seeking new knowledge and experiences that can deepen their understanding and skills.
- **Evolving Practice**: Kabbalah Reiki, like any spiritual practice, evolves over time. Staying updated with the latest developments, techniques, and understandings in the field ensures that practitioners are providing the most effective and relevant services.

Formal Education

- **Advanced Courses**: I would encourage the pursuit of advanced courses in Kabbalah Reiki, including master-level training or specialized workshops that focus on areas such as crystal healing, advanced energy techniques, or integrating other modalities like aromatherapy or sound healing.
- **Certifications and Workshops**: I would recommend obtaining additional certifications in related fields, such as yoga, meditation instruction, or holistic nutrition, to enhance the holistic care provided to clients.

Other Learning Opportunities

- **Books and Publications**: I would encourage to continue your learning through other publications that cover Kabbalah and Reiki and related topics. Remain being the constant researcher.
- **Online Courses**: 'The Centre of Excellence' is an online platform that offers a Diploma in Kabbalah, which I would recommend to those interested in complementing their Kabbalah studies.
- **Seeking Mentors**: Kabbalah Reiki is an advance technique and it is advisable to seek for mentorship from more experienced Kabbalah Reiki masters. Mentors can provide guidance, support, and insights that significantly enhance the learning process. I, mum Lily, am happy to support you in this manner, with both group classes or on a one-to-one basis.

Reflective Practice

- **Journaling**: I would encourage keeping a detailed journal of your Reiki experiences, insights from meditations, client sessions, and personal reflections. This practice can enhance self-awareness and pinpoint areas for further development.
- **Self-Assessment**: I would also recomment to perform regular self-assessment as they help practitioners recognize their strengths and identify areas where they need more knowledge or improvement. This can guide your continuing education choices.

Keeping the Passion Alive

- **Personal Retreats and Sabbaticals**: I would encourage taking personal retreats or sabbaticals focused on deepening these spiritual practices and refreshing your passion for healing work.
- **Exploring New Territories**: Finally, I would like to also encourage to explore new territories in healing and spirituality, such as integrating art or nature into your Reiki practice, to keep your approach fresh and engaging.

Part X

Closing Remarks and Resources

Dear Beloved Souls

As we draw to the close of this journey through the pages of this manual, I hope that you have found guidance, inspiration, and profound insights to enrich your practice and spiritual exploration. Kabbalah Reiki is not merely a technique; it is a pathway to deep healing, spiritual awakening, and the harmonious balance of mind, body, and soul.

Embracing the Journey
Remember, the journey of Kabbalah Reiki is one of continuous growth and learning. Each step you take on this path deepens your connection with the divine and the infinite energies that flow through the universe. Embrace each moment of practice with openness and humility, and always strive to align your actions with the highest good.

Commitment to Practice
I encourage you to commit wholeheartedly to your practice, integrating the teachings and techniques shared in this manual into your daily life. Let the principles of love, light, and healing guide you as you assist others on their paths, and as you navigate your own spiritual journey.

Community and Connection
You are not alone on this journey. Reach out to fellow practitioners, engage with your community, and share your experiences and insights. The strength of our connections with each other can amplify the healing and transformative power of Kabbalah Reiki, creating ripples of positivity and light across the world.

Continuous Learning
Stay curious and open to learning. The fields of Kabbalah and Reiki are vast, and the depths of their wisdom are infinite. Continue to seek out new knowledge, attend workshops, and read widely. Let your intuition and the divine guidance of the universe lead you to deeper understandings and new opportunities for growth.

Closing Blessing
May your journey be filled with light and love. May the wisdom of Kabbalah enrich your soul, and the healing power of Reiki restore your body and spirit. I bless you with clarity, peace, and the unending support of the spiritual realms.

Walk gently, beloved souls, with compassion and mindfulness. Remember that each of you is a beacon of light in a world that yearns for healing and spiritual connection. Hold your light high, and let it guide you ever onwards.

With all my love and blessings,

Mum Lily

About Mum Lily

Greetings and warm wishes. I'm Liliana Cisneros, often referred to as Mum Lily. Originating from the historic realm of Peru, I've made Australia my home for the majority of my existence. Spirituality is the essence of my being and serves as a steadfast pillar in my life.

Gifted with profound recollection, my memories extend beyond the confines of this life and era. This ongoing voyage of recollection and enlightenment is one I embrace with joy.

As a passionate scholar, I delight in imparting the wisdom I acquire on my path. My academic background is comprehensive, with advanced degrees in English and Psychology, and a Bachelor's degree encompassing Social Work, Business, and Music. My expertise spans a range of fields including Education, Languages, Mental Health, and Community Services.

I am well-versed in a variety of interpretative and restorative practices, such as Tarot, Oracle, and Crystal readings, Reiki, Shamanism, Astrology, Numerology, Life Coaching, Counselling, and the study of Kabbalah.

With a keen intellect, my interests are diverse, ranging from singing and culinary arts to exploring the enigmas of extra-terrestrial life. I approach life with resilience and a positive outlook.

My connection to the divine is profound, and I hold a special affinity for working with the Archangels, especially Metatron and Uriel.

It is my honour to guide others to rediscover their innate essence, regain their strength, and shape the destiny they desire.

Namaste,

Mum Lily

Contact Information

 Casa Alhambra Crystal Store
77 Vulture Street - West End - QLD - 4101 - Australia

 www.casaalhambra.com.au
www.mumlily.com

Casa Alhambra
Mum Lily Teaches
Liliana Alva de Cisneros

Mum Lily Teaches

Casa Alhambra
Mum Lily Teaches

casaalhambra@outlook.com
askmumlily@gmail.com

0415-422-007

www.ingramcontent.com/pod-product-compliance
Lightning Source LLC
Chambersburg PA
CBHW081617100526
44590CB00021B/3478